ADVANCE PRAISE FOR

Teaching and Race

"This book offers an in-depth, critical exploration of the potential of a race-themed composition curriculum to encourage racial literacy among college students and their teachers. Lietz's examination of the attitudes, experiences, and struggles of four students, one biracial and three White women, offers key insights into how students come to identify as racialized individuals and how they acknowledge, critique, or accept the privilege that accompanies whiteness. Each chapter follows a student as she evolves or stagnates in her racial literacy development during the course of her undergraduate career, providing an important longitudinal perspective on the racialized identities and experiences of college-aged women. Rather than maintain distance as a researcher, Lietz critically reflects upon her own pedagogical practices and interrogates her positionality as a teacher and a White woman. In doing so, Lietz models the type of self-reflection integral to effective, equitable instruction and highlights the ideological, sociological, and pedagogical considerations we must all take into account to become antiracist educators. *Teaching and Race: How to Survive, Manage, and Even Encourage Race Talk* is an important contribution to the growing body of literature on antiracism in writing studies."

—Mara Lee Grayson, Assistant Professor of English,
California State University, Dominguez Hills;
Author of *Teaching Racial Literacy: Reflective Practices for Critical Writing*

"*Teaching and Race: How to Survive, Manage, and Even Encourage Race Talk* is an important teaching tool and model of reflection on a teacher's own racial subject position for writing teachers of various levels. It offers college and even high school teachers who are white ways to interrogate whiteness, race, and racism in their classrooms with their students. Lietz frames much of her insights gleaned from her teaching and the four students she highlights in the book in ways that I find humble, compassionate, and thoughtful. Her discussion throughout is a good model for how white, female teachers can do important race work both from their own subject positions in the classroom as a teacher and through their readings and activities with students. This is the kind of race work we all can do together in the literacy classroom."

—Asao B. Inoue, Professor and Associate Dean,
College of Integrative Sciences and Arts, Arizona State University;
Author of *Antiracist Writing Assessment Ecologies: Teaching and Assessing for a Socially Just Future*

Teaching and Race

Studies in Composition and Rhetoric

Alice S. Horning

General Editor

Vol. 12

The Studies in Composition and Rhetoric series is part of the Humanities list.
Every volume is peer reviewed and meets
the highest quality standards for content and production.

PETER LANG

New York • Bern • Berlin

Brussels • Vienna • Oxford • Warsaw

Irene Murphy Lietz

Teaching and Race

How to Survive, Manage, and Even Encourage Race Talk

PETER LANG
New York • Bern • Berlin
Brussels • Vienna • Oxford • Warsaw

Library of Congress Cataloging-in-Publication Data

Names: Lietz, Irene Murphy, author.
Title: Teaching and race: how to survive, manage, and
even encourage race talk / Irene Murphy Lietz.
Description: New York: Peter Lang, 2020.
Series: Studies in composition and rhetoric; vol. 12 | ISSN 1080-5397
Includes bibliographical references and index.
Identifiers: LCCN 2020009955 (print) | LCCN 2020009956 (ebook)
ISBN 978-1-4331-7190-1 (hardcover) | ISBN 978-1-4331-8292-1 (paperback)
ISBN 978-1-4331-7191-8 (ebook) | ISBN 978-1-4331-7192-5 (epub)
ISBN 978-1-4331-7193-2 (mobi)
Subjects: LCSH: Racism in higher education—United States. | Race—Study
and teaching (Higher)—United States. | Multicultural education—United
States. | Race relations—Study and teaching (Higher)—United States.
Classification: LCC LC212.42 .L54 2020 (print) | LCC LC212.42 (ebook)
DDC 379.2/6—dc23
LC record available at https://lccn.loc.gov/2020009955
LC ebook record available at https://lccn.loc.gov/2020009956
DOI 10.3726/b15879

Bibliographic information published by **Die Deutsche Nationalbibliothek**.
Die Deutsche Nationalbibliothek lists this publication in the "Deutsche
Nationalbibliografie"; detailed bibliographic data are available
on the Internet at http://dnb.d-nb.de/.

29 Broadway, 18th floor, New York, NY 10006
www.peterlang.com

CONTENTS

ACKNOWLEDGMENTS

Thank you to the students who volunteered for the study that began as the basis of this book and particularly to the four students who participated in the interviews that anchor this book. Their eagerness to learn and their generosity of spirit in learning with me is all a teacher could ever hope for.

To my wise and talented series editor, Alice Horning, and to the staff at Peter Lang, all new friends that I am so grateful to have met: Your professionalism and care for good, important communication is laudatory. Thank you.

To the writers group from Carlow University Pittsburgh, founded by Dr. Katie Hogan, which read early versions of many of these chapters: Sigrid King, Anne Rashid, Jennifer Snyder-Duch, Linda Burns, Melissa Swauger, Sylvia Rohr, and later Judith Toure. Their friendship and encouragement, unwavering faith in my voice, clarity of mind, and patience in teaching me how to research and write qualitatively are among the great gifts of my life.

To Barbara Johnson, Anne Rashid, Addie Morrow, Terri Laws, the YWCA Pittsburgh anti-racism team (formerly the Young Women's Christian Association), and the University of Michigan Program on Intergroup Relations, whose frank conversations about race and willingness to teach me and encourage me in anti-racism work account for both the most obvious and the hardest lessons I've ever learned. Thank you.

To the Brief Daily Sessions (BDS) online group, also founded by Dr. Katie Hogan and Dr. Lisa Brush, which kept me on target and moving through the chapters: Your courage in writing really important work, your tremendous output, your tips and sources, and your gentle support sustained me. Thank you.

To Karyn Sproles, teacher extraordinaire, whose friendship, careful critique, race talk and weekly writing talk helped me sort out almost every word of every chapter, my unbounded gratitude and hope that even as this book is finished, we can still talk.

To my parents, Florence and Jack Murphy, who first encouraged me to care about other people and about education. You were my first writing teachers. Your encouragement of that little grade school kid who wanted to say something to the world through writing is finally seeing fruit. Thank you for all the love, time, and patience that took.

To our son Tom, his wife Erin, our two granddaughters Katherine and Vivian, your interest in, support of, contributions to and sacrifices over the years for this and all my work make me feel so proud and grateful to be your mom, mother-in-law and grandma.

To our daughter Patricia (Patti), another writer (!), your carefully thought out responses to my concerns about the book, the hours of problem-solving and encouragement you provided, and the catch-up lessons in Women's Studies and cultural politics provided crucial support to me in this work. I am always amazed by what you know and how wise beyond your years you have always been.

Patricia, Tom, and Erin, you are all so talented and bring so much to the world and the people you love. I'm so glad you are the people who will be carrying on the spirit of this work in the years after I'm gone. The world is in good hands.

To my immensely patient spouse, Ted, who has brought a fellow writer's understanding of the loves and heartaches, ups and downs of this writing project to our daily lives together: your belief in me and in my need to do this work is so generous and loving. I hope it earns you a really good seat in heaven and that I can support you at least as well. It's hard to give you sufficient acknowledgment and gratitude. Please give me another 45 years to work on that!

Grateful acknowledgment is also made to the following for permission to reproduce the following copyrighted material. Reprinted by permission of the publishers. All rights reserved.

- Lietz, Irene. "'When Do I Cross the Street?' Roberta's Guilty Reflection." *Journal of Expanded Perspectives on Learning* vol. 21, Winter 2015–2016, pp. 100–113.
- Lietz, Irene. "'Anyone Can Hurt You': Elaine's Attack and Defense in Writing About Race." *Language Arts Journal of Michigan* vol. 28, no. 2, Spring 2013, pp. 47–54.

INTRODUCTION

Ever since I was a child I have thought about race because I grew up in the suburbs of Detroit. I say that not to demean Detroit or the suburbs in any way but to verbalize a reality of this area: we all seem to think about race all the time. Other cities have their own version of this phenomenon of "the social problem of the twentieth century [which] is to be the relation of the civilized world to the dark races of mankind," as W.E. B. DuBois predicted (111). But Detroiters are somewhat obsessed with race and how we do it. In a recent three-month period, I read three books set in the city of Detroit that all featured the 1967 race rebellion as a key moment, even as a character. (See Eugenides, J. *Middlesex*; Maraniss, D. *Once in a Great City: A Detroit Story*; and Messer, S. *Grand River and Joy*.) Race and racism are central to the identity and cultural experience of anyone living in the Detroit area.

That's not to say that we actually talk about race in any meaningful or productive way. More often, it is what is not said. People refer to "changing" neighborhoods, schools, strip malls, movie theaters. They debate whose fault it is that the city core—and now the city as a whole—has emptied out, spreading like a spilled can of motor oil in all directions from where it tipped at the hub of the "wheel" near downtown in the 1964 and 1967 uprisings.

Even as today we talk hopefully about the rebirth of the city, how Detroit is "coming back" in a rush of gentrification, restaurants, lofts, casinos, stadiums, and a new two-mile transit system, it's all tinged with a certain cynicism, knowing the corruption and mismanagement that has led to schools almost beyond repair and a too-close view of a poisoned water system just up I-75 in Flint. Race in Detroit, in America, all seems overwhelming and hopeless. But still we hope.

This book comes from a place deep in my heart. When the opportunity arose for my spouse and me to return to Detroit after 30 years away, having grown up, raised our family, and ached at every "Imported from Detroit" Chrysler ad, we were excited to find a home in one of the old, "inner-ring" suburbs that itself was undergoing revival. I wanted a close-in seat from which to work, to see if we could help in the recovery somehow.

I felt I had work to do, both personal and professional. In Pittsburgh for the previous 13 years, I had learned to call my discomfort "liberal White guilt" out of "White privilege" that I had sensed but had not named before. With the help of the YWCA, whose mission is "Eliminating racism, Empowering women," I made some typical White person discoveries at their anti-racism workshops: with pain, I learned I had responsibility for race in America, even if though I personally hadn't owned slaves or even been direct party to the federal lawsuits that my suburban hometown, Warren, MI, had filed to keep "Negroes" from buying in our "safe" neighborhoods. I realized with great regret that I had passed on to our children the same racial fears that I grew up with because, as nice and egalitarian as we believed ourselves to be in the suburbs, none of us really knew anyone different from ourselves and were a little afraid. We lived in a separate world and believed racism was a problem that other people had, that was too big for us to fix personally.

But the YWCA spoke to me; I heard—really heard—for the first time about being a White ally, about working together to equalize opportunity, about creating social change. I read, workshopped, dialogued, and participated in protests with new courage probably born of the desire to end this longstanding guilt, more than anything, although I told myself it was my sense of justice. There is more to this story that I will share later.

This book is about the hope we all carry that things can be different, perhaps even that we can help make that difference a reality by what we do in our classrooms. The point of this book is to give readers—other educators and those who care about education—time and space to consider the specific, different responses of four female students to writing about race while learning to write on the college level. Admittedly, the book only examines four students: three White students and one who identifies as Middle Eastern (Lebanese), who are not inclusive of every race, sex, gender, religion, ethnicity, personality or every response to such a course. This book is not intended as a comprehensive sociological study but instead it is an in-depth, rich portrait of real people readers may recognize from their classrooms, their campuses, their neighborhoods, their families who have real fears, concerns, insights, dreams, and disappointments. These four women represent multiple aspects of student lives and efforts to understand and meaningfully participate in our highly racialized society.

My belief is that by closely examining the students' words and thoughts, readers will become better teachers and even perhaps better people or at least people who are happier with themselves and their way of being in the world. They will (1) see themselves or aspects of themselves in students' responses to race that might otherwise bewilder, embarrass, or even shock them if they occurred in their own classroom; (2) better understand the sources of the students' reactions and concerns so as to respond productively and generously to similar responses in their students; (3) perceive racial identity development as a neglected but crucial facet of student learning that begs for cross-curricular, interdisciplinary attention from all of us; (4) and understand how to adopt greater openness to repairing the inevitable gaps in their own racial identity awareness so as to be able to move outside of their comfort zones in tackling these hot topics with their students who are calling for them to do so.

It is a book for English and Writing instructors, whether in high school, college, or university, who teach writing through empowering student voice. But it may also be for teachers of other disciplines who want to engage their students in skills development in racial and multicultural competency, as an aspect of their disciplinary knowledge.

This book comes from many places, both personal and professional. I sought out the experiences of others, but found my immediate colleagues were focused on other concerns in a small, struggling, teaching-focused liberal arts college, including new research pressures as we transitioned to a university. They had their own overload related to literature and poetry, not writing and race. It felt as if no one understood what I was talking about. Students avoiding race talk? Why are you talking about race in a writing class? Isn't that counseling, sociology, psychology?

When I read Anne Green's "Difficult Stories," I almost heard angels sing. She bravely told the story of her student's cognitive dissonance and racism that was prompted by their service-learning experience in the university's predominantly Black and poor neighborhood. Her White students' withdrew in fright and racial stereotype from the project meant to engage them with the neighboring Black community. Moreover, Green wasn't sure exactly what to do differently, given the realities of lives—her students' and the neighbors'—in a highly racialized society. She knew they were growing in their writing and racial awareness but it was a struggle for them and for her. I was sad for her and her students, but excited as well. There *were* others doing this work and, more importantly, wondering about *how* to best do it. I couldn't stop talking about Green's brave confessions of apparent failure to move her students to critical consciousness or even empathy. "This is the work I would do with a Ph.D. if I could," I relayed to my spouse, my mother, my colleagues. "Then why not do it?" they said.

Why not? Because I was 52 years old with a 30+-year-old master's degree and would be 56 years old when I graduated with a doctorate. Because I'm an English teacher, not a counselor, sociologist, or psychologist. More to the point, because I'm a White person with a good friend who is Black, as the stereotype of liberal Whites goes, but with whom I have never talked about race. And because I'm afraid.

I'm not entirely sure why I decided to move ahead anyway. I suspect I hoped there were intellectual answers to the conundrum of race, a brain-path out of this social and emotional mess that would not go away. Some (many?) of us in higher education live in our heads: we think another article, another study, another research project will yield the missing piece to all knowledge. As I studied for my doctorate, I soon found more colleagues in the books and journals I'd thought had little to say to me about this work. With a vengeance I also collected census data, poverty and educational disparity stats and joblessness analyses, stories of housing and job discrimination, and current events that evidenced race as a continuing social problem that just needed to be surfaced for good people to understand, embrace, and make right. I thought anti-racist change was an intellectual, rational challenge: we all just needed more knowledge to understand and I'd have roomsful of new racial justice advocates. So I found ways to share all this new information with my students; as I learned, they could learn. They wrote about race in the context of learning to write to inform, argue, and persuade. I brought the YWCA and other speakers to my classes, and required readings on race and other social problems. I thought I had some answers.

But not everyone else thought so. Despite my best intentions, students—and my colleagues—did not always think it was a good idea to tackle racial awakening in the context of a writing class. While some went along with the program, as always, many more woke up to resistance, fighting and rejecting both the facts and the logic, even the evidence of their classmates' experiences of difference. Emotions ran high. Every class period was marked by great moments of insight but also painful, even shocking revelations of bias and prejudice. Students were certainly engaged with the topic but at times seemed to feel they were fighting for their very lives. I sometimes felt the same, wondering if this Pandora's box I'd opened was just too much for a first-year writing class, even though their writing was much more interesting and real than before.

Gradually, as I learned more about Whiteness, privilege, and dialogue, I overcame the first shock of their stereotypes and strong judgments and realized they weren't angry at me but at the racial situation in our society. Once I wasn't as afraid of it, their resistance actually began to intrigue me. It came in so many varieties and in many different packages. They obviously needed something more to be able to resolve their resistances to our race work.

Significantly too, even as they struggled against our race talk, students were fully engaged. The race-themed writing course was challenging their identities, who they thought they were and what they thought they knew. It was up close and personal even as it was study of rhetoric and contemporary social issues. To my thinking, it demonstrated the findings of a Harvard study of novice writers that students developed significant writing skill by making a personal commitment to a topic that they might return to repeatedly, crafting a writer identity, engaging with the profession, finding a personal stake and niche (Sommers and Saltz). My students had something to say about race and it related to their future selves, sometimes in the discipline, others just as human beings who were puzzled about the meaning of existence and how to shape their own response to life.

This book is a snapshot of that process. By capturing the reactions and responses of some of the students who took the course, the book closely examines that experience and begins to decipher its meanings. It's an opportunity to hear their voices, their struggles, their hopes and dreams, and to begin to imagine the kinds of changes needed in a writing curriculum, a college or university, even in the field of rhetoric and/or writing studies that might better meet the needs of the students and the teachers like those who are the subject of this story.

Key Questions This Book Will Answer

Ultimately, the point of sharing my narrative and these interviews is to provide just such a rich description of what some might find obvious but which is underdocumented in the literature: (1) White college students bring with them to college all the prejudices of their earlier upbringing that has been reinforced by the "smog" of racism in American society (Tatum 6); (2) biracial and students of color suffer differently in this White-normed environment; (3) students need race education, that is teaching and learning about racial identity and the impacts and contexts of the "White racial frame" in which we live (Feagin); (4) their teachers need this education also; (5) anti-racism is hard work; (6) racism will not end because we wish it would; we need to take direct action against it. This is the argument of this book, addressed in the following questions:

1. How does racial awareness or identity develop, particularly in college-age young people?
2. How do they respond to racial difference?
3. How do their responses play out in the classroom and in academic inquiry into topics that challenge predominant racial stereotypes?
4. Do their responses to and understanding of race and racial identity change over the course of the semester?
5. Do they change over the course of their college career?
6. How does a teacher respond to student responses to talk about race?
7. What are a teacher's responsibilities and/or options in responding to student talk about race?
8. What is a university's responsibility to its students and teachers in a racialized society?

Summary of the Chapters

The chapters can be read in any order but make the most sense as a rhetorical argument and in terms of inter-chapter references if they are read in a linear, numerical order. Note that each chapter ends with a section, "What I Wish I Had Said," that applies some hindsight to the student interviews. I focus particularly on a two-step process I have subsequently learned: to listen compassionately but then challenge the inherent prejudice with several simple questions. Together the active listening and the follow-up questions reliably acknowledge the volatile feelings and misinformation in the room and then facilitate the exploration of some clarifying context drawn from the course content and the diverse experiences among us, the students and teachers.

I summarize all the chapters briefly here for readers with a variety of needs in this moment who want to decide how (or whether) to read the book.

Chapter 1 How to Survive, Manage, and Even Encourage Race Talk

Students, like most White people, don't intend to be racist but lack support from teachers, schools, and their other social institutions in understanding their own racial identities and the differences of others around them. Similarly, for a variety of reasons, the teacher's response to a racially insensitive comment generally falls within the White racial frame (Feagin), that is it reinforces White norms, again without recourse to more racially aware narratives or the skills to manage hot topics, like race. The book offers deep listening followed by some questions that, as illustrated in Chapters 2–6, could interrupt and thoughtfully transform an offensive or misinformed moment into a learning dialogue, answering the perennial teacher question, "What do I say when …?" The questions offered for use are: (1) What is your story? Where did that reaction come from? (2) Does anyone else have a different experience? (3) Does anyone know the history of that term/situation? (4) Where does the reading/film say that? And (5) Has anyone seen any data related to that idea/situation?

Chapter 2 Methodology and Literature: Does Anyone Know the History of That Term/Situation?

The chapter describes the methodology of the IRB-approved, qualitative, longitudinal study of four students who participated in my race-themed first-year writing classes and a sampling of the literature that grounds the argument of the book and the analysis of the student interviews. The argument of the book is that students and their teachers suffer from the prejudices taught to them early in childhood, derived and reinforced by the White racial frame of our historically racialized U.S. society. College classrooms can be sites of racial encounter, particularly if the curriculum includes discussion about or study of race as a social identity. The classroom is an opportunity to explore racial identity in ways that enable both students and teachers to learn about and enact an ally identity, but all participants need to understand how to support such exploration and to feel confident of institutional support for this difficult social justice work.

Chapter 3 Annabell

Annabell is an eager, smart learner who wants to engage fully in the subject at hand, particularly when it stirs her sense of justice. She dives into the intellectual challenge of crafting a new identity that better acknowledges the continuing existence of racism and its privilege, but rejects her association with it, typifying an incomplete accommodation to this new identity. Ironically, her differentiating herself becomes her activism by the time she is a college senior in ways I find very reminiscent of myself as instructor. Thus together, she and I illustrate an intellectualized activism that shapes a new if sometimes incomplete anti-racist White identity.

Chapter 4 Roberta

Roberta epitomized for me the White student—or teacher—who believes it important to call out racism when she sees it and to name the evil among us so that we have some hope of someday eliminating it. Yet in her senior year of college, she seemed to be treading water in the same racial identity place she described in her first year, that is she could not imagine herself acting against racism in any public way. I now believe that she and I, as well as other White people in the class, were caught in the gap between what we came to see as necessary revision of our White identities and our emotional attachment to our past image of ourselves. The difficulties that Roberta faced are not only symptomatic of her courageous battle with White socialization but provide a clarion call for us all to do better by her and all of our students.

Chapter 5 Elaine

The fear in Elaine's eyes seemed to magnify their whites, yet there was a perpetual smile on her lips as she sat in the chair next to my desk in the privacy of my office. She clearly did not want to alienate me with her harsh racist words but she felt driven to make her point: I wasn't understanding her life experience. She wanted to know, what did any of this talk about racism have to do with the essays we were writing in our first-year composition class? Why couldn't we all just get along and stop talking about race? It only made things worse between the "colored" people and the rest of us. She also told of the fear she felt on the city bus that she perceived as filled with Black people who regarded her and her boyfriend with fear and suspicion as she clutched his arm. Where does this fear come from? How does it work? What could I understand that would help students respond to this fear in a constructive manner? Teachers need to recognize these fears, understand their sources, and find ways to incorporate their constituent resistance into the learning experience.

Chapter 6 Madeline

Madeline could talk an arm off the Venus de Milo. A student who identified as Middle Eastern but appeared White, due to her Irish heritage, she loved the opportunity to "finally" talk about race, racism, and White privilege in America. It seemed everyone at school and in Pittsburgh lived in a different world that didn't see or "get" what she thought was obvious, common sense; she was out of place, out of sync and alone, and no one would listen to her protest about this situation. As the only student of color in this project and one of few in the class itself, Madeline's stories and opinions provide insights on the student who brings to the classroom an experience of difference, causing her to struggle to find her footing, her voice, and her identity. How can a critical classroom pedagogy meet the divergent, even oppositional needs of the students of color who are already keenly aware of the failure of our society to adequately grapple with racial inequity? At the same time, how can the classroom educate and hold accountable the White students, their teachers and institutions, who fearfully resist awareness of racism and their complicity in maintaining a "white racial frame" (Feagin)?

Chapter 7 Next Steps

At this point in the book, readers may be asking, "But where do I start?" In the first section of this chapter, DiAngelo responds, "How do you not know?" She shows readers how their White fragility that has caused them to turn aside rather than see what must be done. DiAngelo offers readers manageable activities to help them get rid of whatever is in the way of seeing the next steps. In section two, Asao Inoue challenges readers (and me) to pay attention to the embedded racism in the English language and in the field. He argues teachers need to let go of Standard Edited American English as the only standard by which to judge students' ideas so that educators can free themselves, students, and institutions from "the steel cage of White supremacy." The story of my student James suggests both the problem and solution. Section three features Mara Grayson's racial literacy curriculum ideas from small to large, an approach for every size ambition. Finally, I suggest readers find a buddy or better yet, *buddies* to help make their hopes and visions really happen.

A Note About Capitalization and Terminology with a Cordial Invitation

Although this book follows Modern Language Association (MLA) style, MLA does not comment on the capitalization of racial or ethnic groups. So, in this book on this matter, I have chosen to abide by the American Psychological Association (APA). In its listing, "Racial and Ethnic Identity," APA simply says, "Racial and ethnic groups are designated as proper nouns and are capitalized. Therefore, use *Black* and *White* instead of *black* and *white* (the use of colors to refer to other human groups currently is considered pejorative and should not be used)" (italics original). Thus, in this book, readers will see capitalization for African American, Black, White, and Whiteness, except where a quoted author has not capitalized. However, there is more to consider about this choice.

Notably when I began this racial identity project in the early part of this century, I was advised that the standard was to capitalize African American and sometimes Black but not White. This idea aligns with a journalistic standard at *The New York Times* and the Columbia Journalism Review (Perlman). But, consider more closely the justification provided by the DiversityInc. Blogger that Perlmann quotes who says, "I do not believe 'white,' needs to be capitalized because people in the majority don't think of themselves that way."

That damaging belief in the normalcy and transparency of Whiteness is precisely one of the points of this book. White people are often unaware that they too have a race in our racialized society. Their resistance to being called White is a tactic of the color-blindness that reinforces the White privilege of racial dominance. Anti-racist rhetorician Krista Ratcliffe explains that the effects of such denial of ownership of a racial identity are, "It allows whites to become voyeurs of race, it targets non-white people as the only ones for whom race is an issue, and consequently, it enables whiteness to remain invisible and unarticulated as a 'color' or, more precisely, as a racial coding that intersects gender and other cultural categories" (Ratcliffe 89). Such invisibility of how Whiteness operates has cloaked American history's cruel and bloody White supremacy in righteousness, fairness, and opportunity for all when it is in fact a "*dual* and *dueling* history of racial progress and simultaneous progression of racism," as historian Ibram Kendi (x) so shockingly documents (italics original).

White denial of and lack of accountability for that history is why I have chosen to capitalize White and Whiteness. I want to call out the reality of White racial identity as a cultural and political force, thus equally recognizing all racial terms as "social classifications rather than innate biological characteristics" (Grayson xvii). This naming of White, in particular, is an effort to remove the privileged hidden normalization of "White" as the standard against which all other groups are seen as different and inferior. It is, perhaps, a way people can begin to see and hear each other truly as persons with common needs and desires.

In addition, as explained elsewhere, three of the four student interviews included in this book are from students who identify as White, but one identifies as Mediterranean or Lebanese, as well as Irish or White. As I discovered in her interview, it is her Lebanese heritage that she holds most strongly and feels sets her apart as an outsider. Almost at the same time as that interview, the United States Census Bureau began considering the addition of a separate Middle Eastern, North African, or Arab (MENA) option to the current five race categories on the national census form (White, Black or African American, American Indian or Alaska Native, Asian, and Native Hawaiian or Other Pacific Islander) as well as Some Other Race (U.S. Census Bureau "Race"). Census Bureau research has indicated that MENA members have been identifying as White when there is not a MENA option (U.S. Census Bureau "Research") and the Bureau wants to correct that behavior. But National Public Radio (NPR) reports that other community members prefer MENA to be categorized as ethnicity rather than race, and as a result, MENA will not appear on the 2020 census (Wang). This government and internal community struggle demonstrates the socially constructed nature of both race and ethnicity, rather than any essential biology or geography. It also reflects the distress of Otherness and the White normativity that complicates all social interaction, including that my Lebanese student suffered, as readers will see. Although certainly the four students in this book are not representative of all students or even all White people, their struggles with the complexity of race and racialization in our society definitely are symptomatic of the ongoing pain and many dilemmas created by our society's perverse need to categorize people.

As such, I invite readers to share in this complex story about racial identity, to hear these voices, to consider them from the perspective of their own experience and that of their students, institutions, and colleagues. Many teachers have been trying for a long time to have conversations about the difficulty of living and teaching in a racialized society. I hope that this book will resonate, inform, and encourage teachers to seek out other ways and opportunities to talk about race, to tell their stories, and to provide more space for others to tell theirs in ways that help everyone move towards greater justice.

Works Cited

DiAngelo, Robin. *White Fragility*. Beacon Press, 2018.

Du Bois, W.E.B. "The Present Outlook for the Dark Races of Mankind." *The Problem of the Color Line at the Turn of the Twentieth Century*, edited by Nahum Dimitri Chandler. Fordham University, 2014, pp. 111–137.

Feagin, Joe R. *The White Racial Frame: Centuries of Racial Framing and Counter-Framing*. Routledge, 2010.

Grayson, Mara Lee. *Teaching Racial Literacy: Reflective Practices for Critical Writing*. Rowman & Littlefield, 2018.

Green, Ann E. "Difficult Stories: Service-Learning, Race, Class and Whiteness." *College Composition and Communication*, vol. 55, no. 2, 2003, pp. 276–301.

Inoue, Asao B. "How Do We Language So People Stop Killing Each Other, or What Do We Do About White Language Supremacy?." *Conference on College Composition and Communication*, Keynote address, 14 March 2019.

Kendi, Ibram X. *Stamped from the Beginning: The Definitive History of Racist Ideas in America*. Nation Books, 2016.

Perlman, Merrill. "Black and White: Why Capitalization Matters." *Columbia Journalism Review*, 2015. 22 June 2019.

"Racial and Ethnic Identity." *Publication Manual of the American Psychological Association*, edited by Gary R. VandenBos. American Psychological Association, 2010, pp. 75–76.

Ratcliffe, Krista. "Rhetorical Listening: A Trope for Interpretive Invention and a 'Code of Cross-Cultural Conduct'." *College Composition and Communication*, vol. 51, no. 2, 1999, pp. 195–224.

Sommers, Nancy and Laura Saltz. "The Novice as Expert: Writing the Freshman Year." *College Composition and Communication*, vol. 56, no. 1, 2004, pp. 124–149.

Tatum, Beverly Daniel. *"Why Are All the Black Kids Sitting Together in the Cafeteria?" And Other Conversations About Race*. Basic Books, 2003.

U.S. Census Bureau. "Race." U.S. Census Bureau 23 Jan 2018 https://www.census.gov/topics/population/race/about.html. Accessed 28 June 2019.

—. "Research to Improve Data on Race and Ethnicity." U.S. Census Bureau 6 March 2017 https://www.census.gov/about/our-research/race-ethnicity.html. Accessed 28 June 2019.

Wang, Hansi Lo. "No Middle Eastern or North African Category on 2020 Census, Bureau Says." *National Public Radio*, 29 Jan 2018.

· 1 ·

HOW TO SURVIVE, MANAGE, AND EVEN ENCOURAGE RACE TALK

In her incisive, insightful book, *Rethinking Racism: Emotion, Persuasion, and Literacy in an All-White High School*, Jennifer Trainor's introduction to her argument forecasts the structure of this first chapter. Speaking of White student racism, she says it

> … does not necessarily arise from a need or desire to protect White privilege, from ignorance of oppression, or from lack of exposure to difference. As long as the origins of racism are seen in these terms, curricular and pedagogical responses aimed at ameliorating racism—everything from multicultural exposure to difference to critical interrogations of Whiteness and privilege—will be ineffective … [R]emedying [student racism] requires attention to the private, idiosyncratic, associative meanings of race for students, to the institutional contexts of schooling that inadvertently provide emotional scaffolding for racist discourses, and to the relationship between these two as they come together in the classroom. (3–4)

Trainor, an associate professor of composition studies, lays out the three-part focus of her call for change and now mine: students, teachers, and the schools. As the student interviews in this book illustrate, students in our high school, college, and university classes across the disciplines are struggling to make sense of the racism that they have come to see on our campuses, in society, and in themselves. Until this encounter with new information and experience, they have been unaware of the White racial frame, to use sociologist Joe Feagin's term, that has influenced their earliest interactions with family members and people of color, as well as the color of the peoples they were schooled with in a curriculum that bestows honor and attention on White people often at the expense of the rest of the story about the accomplishments and the oppression of people of color.

In terms of the student focus of this book, each of the chapters examines the students' particular personal responses to a race-themed course, their words and attitudes, in the light of Ratcliffe's catalogue of resistances (138–139), Baxter Magolda's student development theory, Trainor's focus on emotion and race, as well as others. Readers may recognize that while not comprehensive, their comments are fairly universal and generalizable to many other students in our classrooms, as well as to faculty and staff in some cases. Each story and analysis serves as the starting point to the reader's implicit question, "So what can I do about that kind of comment when it happens in my classroom?" Sometimes, as in the case of Madeline and Elaine, I confess ineffective teacher responses or at least my sense of inadequacy in fully supporting the learning efforts of Annabelle and Roberta. Please consider these as object lessons in what not to do. So as not to leave readers hanging on a limb, each chapter also provides a brief consideration of how they might respond to such a student generally using strategies that might seem to contradict each other but recognize both the emotional scaffolding, to use Trainor's term (3–4), and the informational needs implicit in every student's story: compassionate listening and critical challenge.

But, I regret, these chapters are not a complete how-to package. Toxic classroom environments and campus life microaggressions are not a student problem, that is "fixing" the students will not make the problem(s) go away. Included in an institutional critique and reform agenda has to be a compassionate indictment of our teacher selves, myself included. As mentioned in the Intro and discussed in Chapter 2, we are products and promulgators of a system that fails to prepare us to live together with respect and dignity across the color lines. As Trainor indicates above, racism is largely not about people with malicious intent. There is no point in wasting time on blame or guilt. If we become as defensive as many of our students do, we are all stuck. We need to do our own remedial homework. But this work is not on our shoulders alone.

This chapter will also begin to name the support we need from our workplaces to make greater justice more possible and sustainable. What is the role and responsibility of the institutions within which we teachers live and work?

As Chapter 2 and some of the student interviews suggest, our high schools, colleges, and universities need to recognize and respond to the pedagogical crisis that a racialized society creates in our classrooms. To do less, to continue to omit or ignore that work, will ensure the continued failure of our schools to adequately prepare students to build and maintain sustainable communities, cities, even nations.

Starting with Us: Why Teachers Fear Race Talk and How They Avoid It

Teachers may fear allowing or focusing discussion on race for multiple reasons. Chief among these is their own fear of talking about race. Sue reports on the work of Pasque as well as his own work with Torinio: "Despite this strong belief [in the value of diversity], most teachers report making few changes to facilitate race talk, and feel uncomfortable and unprepared to deal with potentially heated exchanges on the topic" (Sue 65). When faced with a microaggression or potential confrontation about race or identity, Sue notes that teachers generally respond with various kinds of avoidance (cognitive, emotional, behavioral) and take one of five damaging courses of (non)action: do nothing, sidetrack the conversation, appease the participants, terminate the discussion, and/or become defensive (Sue 230–234). As discussed in Chapter 2, educators are subject to the assaults and influences of a pervasively racialized society just like everyone else. No one is immune; we are all "smog breathers," to repeat Tatum's metaphor (Tatum 6). Our knowledge, on some level, of our compromised abilities to function freely and without bias makes us fearful of the moments in which we might let slip our carefully managed demeanor on the "front stage" (Houts Picca and Feagin) in mixed groups or in situations where we are called upon to talk about race, even in homogenous classrooms.

Teachers are often afraid of feeling ambushed by student race talk and risking betrayal of their own involuntary racism, and for White teachers, their "White fragility", as DiAngelo names it. Because we are captives of our socialization into

> … a deeply internalized sense of superiority that we either are unaware of or can never admit to our selves, we become highly fragile in conversations about race. We consider a challenge to our racial worldviews as a challenge to our very identities as good, moral people. Thus, we perceive any attempt to connect us to the system of racism as an unsettling and unfair moral offense. The smallest amount of racial stress

> is intolerable—the mere suggestion that being White has meaning often triggers a range of defensive responses. These include emotions such as anger, fear, and guilt and behaviors such as argumentation, silence, and withdrawal from the stress-inducing situation. These responses work to reinstate White equilibrium as they repel the challenge, return our racial comfort, and maintain our dominance within the racial hierarchy. I conceptualize this process as *White fragility*. Though White fragility is triggered by discomfort and anxiety, it is born of superiority and entitlement. White fragility is not weakness per se. In fact, it is a powerful means of White racial control and the protection of White advantage. (2)

I recognize my own fragility. I have felt that rush of adrenaline and embarrassment at comments that reveal the participants' overt and/or more subtle racism; I have been paralyzed by fear of speaking out and speaking up, as my pulse pounded in my temples. In other words, I have been triggered by my students as I am sure my students have been triggered by other students in our class or even me, that is set off emotionally by someone else's words. Adams, Bell, and Griffin, in their seminal *Teaching for Diversity and Social Justice*, identify emotional triggers as individual or institutional acts that cause a feeling of psychological threat, either for ourselves or for another social group. How are emotional triggers and student (teacher) resistance to race talk related? People, especially teachers who are invested in managing classroom learning, want to avoid these triggered moments when they feel out of control or on the verge of not being able to control their emotions appropriately. They want ways to step back from their discomfort, panic, and/or cognitive dissonance that arises when they encounter racist talk or even legitimate but foreign perspectives on race and others' racial identity experiences. Adams, et al note a range of responses that include familiar but often ineffective strategies, such as leaving the site, avoidance, silence, attack, internalization, rationalization, confusion, shock, and misinterpretation (Adams et al. Appendix 3B). For many instructors, it seems suicidal to introduce a hot topic like race or to allow discussion to meander in that direction, the stuff of teacher nightmares at 2:00 a.m.

Some teachers lately and bravely raised this spectre at a recent local professional conference where I presented my experience of co-facilitating a faculty-staff intergroup dialogue study group. The English-teacher audience completed an anonymous self-report inventory of their confidence levels that they could respond in affirmative ways to microaggressions in their classroom. I had developed the inventory informally from Derald Wing Sue's list of

"Successful Strategies: Eleven Potentially Positive Actions," (234–244). The first two items are my own creation, followed by those based on Sue.

Self-Inventory Please respond to each of the following statements by indicating your level of confidence that you could perform the following actions in a classroom or workplace setting (4 = very confident, 0 = no confidence).

1. I can recognize and respond to racial or other social identity stereotypes.

   4................3................2................1................0

2. I welcome talk about race or other social identities in my classes.

   4................3................2................1................0

3. I understand the history of and feel comfortable in my own racial and cultural identity.

   4................3................2................1................0

4. I can acknowledge and be open to admitting my own racial biases.

   4................3................2................1................0

5. I am comfortable and open to discussing topics of race and racism.

   4................3................2................1................0

6. I understand the meanings of emotions that emerge in race talk.

   4................3................2................1................0

7. I know how to validate and facilitate discussion of such feelings in race talk.

   4................3................2................1................0

8. I seek to control the process and not the content of race talk.

   4................3................2................1................0

9. I know how to unmask difficult dialogue through process observations and interventions.

   4...............3...............2...............1...............0

10. I do not allow a difficult dialogue to be brewed in silence.

   4...............3...............2...............1...............0

11. I understand differences in communication styles in race talk.

   4...............3...............2...............1...............0

12. I foresee, forewarn, plan, and purposefully instigate race talk.

   4...............3...............2...............1...............0

13. In race talk, I validate, encourage, and express admiration and appreciation for participants to speak when it is unsafe to do so.

   4...............3...............2...............1...............0

When I asked the conference session participants how they felt in completing the inventory, there was a moment of silence, and then, "Uncomfortable." "Unprepared." "Anxious." And then, surprisingly, "Fired up!" Once they processed what the last respondent said, the others were grateful for her positive energy: she was eager to have finally the chance to think together about approaches that might help us all. We had a brief, productive session, including another instructor's valuable input described in the next section, and several people approached me after the presentation to share more about their own experiences and concerns.

We teachers need more such moments to talk to each other about how to talk about race in our classes and institutions. As I have talked to my colleagues about the writing of this book, most have expressed similar feelings. The level of anxiety is high about where and how to get help in this matter. The timing is actually perfect. Just as we come to a so-called minority majority as a society, more and more of us are resolved to find ways to meet this challenge. The reality, though, is that we need help, from each other and from our institutions. This book is a step in that direction, a conversation starter between the reader and the many scholars I've cited, as well as myself.

Compassionate Listening, Critical Challenge, and More

Another of the college instructors who attended the conference session I mentioned earlier asked a question that motivated much of our discussion. Without detracting from anything I had presented about the value of a faculty-staff intergroup dialogue study group, he asked simply, "But what do I *say* when students say something racist in class?" He went on to clarify that the students do not mean to be racist but often lack the vocabulary or background to even enter a "hot topic" discussion without being offensive in some way. As the interviews in this book indicate, this phenomenon is not uncommon. In fact, it's what most of us fear and is often the reason teachers hesitate to even open the opportunity for dialogue about race.

My heart went out to the college instructor at the conference immediately. I had been in his shoes and it was clear that many others in the room had been there too. I told him that my go-to response to students who are feeling the need to defend themselves as good White people is, "Why do you say that? What experience have you had that makes you say it that way?" Strategically, that gives me some time to calm my own defenses and fears, to take a breath before challenging their misinformation, and think about my response to the emotion in the student comment before trying to engage their brains in a logical rebuttal of facts. In a rhetorical move of compassion for the way our segregated society has set us all up to struggle with difference, I want to invite the students to step back from a fearful precipice and tell the story that may anchor—and give me clues into—their mindset, or actually, their heart-set.

The teacher's question made me realize that I was carrying around a list of such questions and strategies that helped me structure what used to be a scary, avoid-at-all-costs moment in my classes. The basic approach is to engage the speakers first, to give the space to tell their own story so that they feel heard, their emotions recognized. But it's a two-step: when the speakers feel a little validated as people—not necessarily their words or ideas—there is an opening for a critical challenge. I can ask, "Has anyone had a different experience with that?" or "What is the history of that term?" or "What does the reading (or film) have to say about that?" or "Has anyone come across any data that challenges that?" In other words, engaging us all in a few moments of compassionate listening can shift the tone and open (or keep open) the dialogue about the issues that we all wish we knew how to talk about together.

Thus, a moment of acknowledgment: I have not consciously appropriated my questions and strategies from any one source. To my knowledge, they are a sort of amalgamation and classroom application based on my teaching experience and the work of many other social justice teachers and scholars. As readers have no doubt recognized, my work is built on the work of many others, many of whom I discuss in Chapter 2. But that provenance has brought me to this new, pragmatic place.

To summarize, the approach starts with …

1. What is your story? Where did that reaction come from? Then …
2. Does anyone else have a different experience?
3. Does anyone know the history of that term/situation?
4. Where does the reading/film say that?
5. Has anyone seen any data related to that idea/situation?

As I said, this approach and these questions are not revolutionary or even unique. Readers may have posed similar questions in other settings. In fact, these questions recall but are a more compact form of the "Useful Questions for Dialogue Facilitation" developed by the Program on Intergroup Relations (IGR) at the University of Michigan. Intergroup Dialogues (IGD) is

> … a face-to-face facilitated learning experience that brings together students from different social identity groups over a sustained period of time to understand their commonalities and differences, examine the nature and impact of societal inequalities, and explore ways of working together toward greater equality and social justice. (Zuniga et al. 2)

IGD's combination of "content learning," "structured interaction," and "facilitative guidance" over a semester-long college class has been shown over its 20+ year history to be "associated positively with a host of measures of cognitive, sociocognitive, diversity attitudes, democratic sentiments, and voting behavior," as Pat Gurin notes in the forward to one of the facilitator handbooks (Maxwell et al. xviii). Of course, the questions that facilitators use in debriefing the IGD experiences are key to their remarkable success, but IGD's structure as a class makes it difficult to utilize as an intervention in a different class, as discussed later.

This book's compassionate listening-critical challenge approach could also be considered an application of Ratcliffe's list of resistances (138–139) that she directly teaches to her students for their use in recognizing and naming their own responses to hot-button issues. The questions might be used before the "naming" of a behavior, laying the dialogic groundwork for debriefing and self-reflection afterwards. Similarly, the approach can serve as a way into Sue's list of successful strategies for developing and acting on critical race consciousness (233–234) that were the basis of the self-inventory, mentioned earlier.

My point is that the two-step compassionate listening and critical challenge, applied to a racial dialogue or to a discussion that teeters on the brink of an umanageable morass, creates thinking space for me in potentially explosive and hurtful emotional terrain. The reason the approach works in the classroom, even and especially when the tone is getting heated and honest, is that it activates the critical thinking about emotions and personal experiences, bridging personal experience and learned emotion with data and evidence that can be brought to bear in the discussion. In Chapter 2 and numerous other points in this book, I discuss Trainor's finding of the emotional disconnect that the high school students who were the focus of her research study experienced between their class's critical race study and the color blindness that their schooling generally taught as the appropriate American civic response to identity stereotypes and inequity. The approach works because it makes room in the dialogue for race-inflected emotions in the context of the rational, fact-based elements. Brought together in a dialogic setting instead of in Cartesian opposition, emotions *with* facts can create a paradigmatic shift in a critical inquiry about race and identity.

In this way, the two-step mimics an aspect of the design of the University of Michigan Intergroup Dialogues (IGD) model, giving "explicit attention to content and process" and touching on at least two of the three "dimensions of learning—cognitive, affective, and behavioral" (Zuniga et al. 21).

Compassionate listening with critical challenge draws students back to the cognitive content of the course while also making space for their previous formal and informal learning and experience, that is, the emotional process. The approach gives pedagogical structure to an exploration of the volatile mix of the past (emotions) and the present (factual content).

As a close cousin or even offspring of IGD, the two-step begins to "help surface these [social identity bias] issues and to help participants work through them" as University of Michigan professor Mark Chesler explains the task in "The Role of Facilitators," an unpublished handout from the Program on Intergroup Relations' annual Intergroup Dialogues Institute . Although referring to active work on social justice issues in general, not the two-step approach discussed in this book, Chesler names the specific mechanisms for surfacing bias in the following bulleted list, activities also generated by compassionate listening with critical challenge:

- Surface stereotypes
- Explore areas of discomfort
- Challenge misinformation and ignorance
- Access and interpret available sources of knowledge in texts/research
- Mediate antagonism and distrust
- Surface underlying (or unstated) differences and conflicts
- Work target-agent issues within groups and across groups
- Help participants understand multiple social group identities
- Help participants understand the structural origins and dynamics of inequality/oppression/privilege
- Ask participants to be specific about their experiences, views, and their implications
- Help participants move between the "in here" and the "out there," between the personal and the abstract, between the mind and the heart
- Invite participants to join alliances to act for change

The Intergroup Dialogues (IGD), as theorized, practiced, and studied by the Program on Intergroup Relations at the University of Michigan, provides a richer, fuller pedagogy for the development of critical consciousness than my triage approach does. I have incorporated IGD readings and hands-on activities, as learned at the annual Institute, in several of my composition classes, as well as in other formats and settings. I am a fan and deeply appreciate its power and scholarly legacy.

But most of us find ourselves in courses and settings that are not set up for Intergroup Dialogues due to constraints (time, curriculum, culture, professional development, and more). I will not suggest using the two-step as an alternative to structured dialogue. It would not work very well outside of a "sustained and intimate engagement across differences" (Zuniga et al. 20) that is a setting that allows participants to trust the group during uncomfortable encounters with other truths. Given that assumption, though, compassionate listening with critical challenge can be a tool for the instructor faced with an immediate teachable moment that she doesn't want to let slip away. In that way, the two-step can be a passport into important and timely race talk that the teacher might not otherwise undertake or permit.

In writing this book, I realized that I use the two-step to activate the mechanisms that help surface bias, as Chesler puts it, in my classes and workshops. But I didn't start there. As suggested by the "What I Wish I Had Said" at the end of each chapter in this book, I was not really prepared to respond to the students included in this book in this way. I wasn't ready yet to understand what I needed to do and why. That only came later, with the help of many more knowledgeable colleagues and friends, particularly friends of color.

What I'm saying now, which may be obvious, is that (1) it is important for teachers to understand their own stances as they do this work, (2) it takes time for teachers to do their own personal "homework," and (3) teachers need to be tutored in this work. White people—students, faculty, and staff—need to understand their Whiteness and how to overcome the White racial frame (Feagin), further discussed in Chapter 2. Depending upon their experiences, people of color—students, faculty, and staff—may also need a structural understanding of the White racial frame. People all need time, space, and guidance to learn to talk with each other through, not around, their differences and to counter the hegemonic influences of Whiteness that pervade their social lives, as well as their understandings of themselves. This work is a personal responsibility, one that many see as part of the job and professionalism. But teachers cannot do it adequately or sustainably without institutional support.

How and Why Schools, Colleges, and Universities Can (Must) Help Teachers

As Robert Eddy and Victor Villanueva assert in their *Language and Power Reader*, "That bigotries are not what they used to be is not the same as progress; that we can toss the word *diversity* into institutions is not the same as addressing structural problems" (6). The hard work of teaching about race in the context of high school or college classes cannot happen in an institutional vacuum. As discussed in Chapter 2, teachers have a social, civic, and pedagogical responsibility to prepare students to be able to function competently, even comfortably, in a diverse but race-conscious society.

Moreover, the pay-offs for teaching about race are big. The University of Michigan's legal defense of its race-conscious admissions policies included expert testimony from psychology and women's studies professor Patricia Gurin in which she concluded that students engaged in diversity experiences, like the Intergroup Dialogues curriculum, made different choices about where they lived and worked, had more diverse friend groups, and were more likely to vote to redress racial inequality than their peers who did not participate in such diversity work (Gurin). In other studies, Gurin found that college students with significant and extended diversity experiences like intergroup dialogues "were living racially and ethnically integrated lives in the post-college world … This confirms that the long-term pattern of segregation noted by many social scientists can by broken by diversity experiences during college." Kuh, et al. have further documented the learning gains inherent in pedagogy that actively engages students in the exploration of diverse perspectives.

In other words, a university commitment to supporting in-depth diversity experiences as part of the college education has a significant impact on both the student learning outcomes in college and on the social and civic behavior of students after college. But it takes an institutional commitment to making this kind of diversity experience possible for students and teachers, a permeating mission that can counter external social and political pressures from a society entrenched in a White racial frame, as sociologist Feagin has named it, and all its punishing, privileging race-conscious milieu.

Without such institutional awareness and commitment, the road for instructors is rocky. Examples of the difficulty of living and teaching about race without that institutional support are not hard to find. In a heart-wrenching narrative about being "out on a limb" as an instructor of color in the college classroom, Bonnie TuSmith tells her story and that of many others in which students dismissed, discounted, and insulted their teachers of color because they were not part of the White majority at the university, especially when they taught about race and privilege. Quoting conclusions from a three-year study by Trzyna and Abbott of students in an ethnic literature course, she notes the emotional and ultimately professional consequences of engaging students in race talk:

> Teaching about race, gender, poverty, and other social and cultural differences is fraught with obstacles, and high on the list of those obstacles is grief, that complex bundle of hostility, sorrow, denial, bargaining, and other feelings that can manifest itself in many forms, including student protests … (qtd. inTuSmith 113)

Besides the day-to-day challenges of engaging students in study they find so emotionally disruptive, TuSmith describes the predictably negative effects on student evaluations of people of color who teach about social justice topics: "Most students do not associate emotional turmoil with a 'good class'" and punish the instructor with low evaluations, which "renders the uniform use of course evaluations problematic. In my experience, the system is open to abuse" (113–114). As a result, TuSmith and others suffered difficulties with timely promotion, making instructor willingness or even ability to teach about race much less likely, no matter the mission of the educational institution.

While not the same as the effects on instructors of color, simply teaching counterhegemonic narratives also generally engenders negative student reactions. In a post-election 2016 innovation, emboldened conservative students developed a professor watch-list "to expose and document college professors who discriminate against conservative students, promote anti-American values, and advance leftist propaganda in the classroom" (Knott). Among those listed were two Notre Dame professors:

> One is philosophy professor Gary Gutting, who is on the list, according to the watch list website, because he wrote that the country's "permissive gun laws are a manifestation of racism." That came from a 2015 analysis about gun laws that Gutting wrote for the New York Times. The other is Iris Outlaw, director of Multicultural Student Programs and Services at the Catholic university. She is on the list, the website says, because she "taught a 'White privilege' seminar that pledged to help students acknowledge and understand their White privilege." (Strauss)

Though not a new idea, McCarthy-like watch lists have a chilling effect on the willingness of instructors of any color in any era to teach about hot topics, race included. At the same time, pundits are noting "the feel of a dispossessed youth rising up" in the alt-right (Kovaleski et al.) and "The beast of far-right populism is reawakening"(Potok). Teachers at all levels must feel free and empowered to respond with factual critical analysis and to be able to show their students how to understand what is happening in their world and how to respond in civil, socially responsible ways.

But as the participants in my earlier mentioned conference session noted, teachers at all levels are not prepared to take on this role. Rosenberg has found in her extensive work with pre-service K-12 teachers that they are "students from predominantly White teacher education programs who have struggled to give voice to their experience of coming to terms with educational biographies that were, for the most part, colored by privilege" (258). McIntyre's study of White teachers indicts teaching and teacher education programs for their inability to accommodate student differences and racism in our society.

> The participants found it extremely difficult to make connections between societal structures, institutions, and their own positionalities as White teachers. And when they did make those connections, there was a tendency to minimize the resulting oppression for students of color, blame other Whites for the damage done, or both ... (130)

Teachers may not be to blame for their difficulty in dealing with race in the classroom but they have a responsibility, McIntyre contends, to critically assess their teaching in the light of known information about institutional racism, whether or not that was part of their upbringing. Otherwise, her study concludes, teachers risk practicing a "caring without critique discourse that uncritically accepts the status quo," and "limit[s] the construction of knowledge and privilege[s] the dominant discourse.". If teachers cannot or will not become informed about racism and craft their teaching in ways that respond to its effects, they risk damaging their students of color as well as their White students and maintain systemic racism.

There is more evidence of the power of teachers to disrupt racism in education and thus change our society, if they are willing and take action. Goodburn calls for teachers and researchers to understand how Whiteness is a privileging color in our classrooms and society, and "how we, as teachers and researchers, read and write our students as 'raced' texts" (Goodburn 72). Pimental's indictment of composition classrooms notes the fear and lack of social or institutional support for countering underlying the White European American (WEA) norm and its resulting de facto racist pedagogy. To fail, to be unable or afraid to interrogate our own privilege and Whiteness and its many impacts on our teaching and our positioning of our students, leaves us in an oppressive position, as Gilyard describes: "Not to [deconstruct race] in the contexts in which we work, is to confirm the prevailing discourse and to be implicated in the maintenance of an exploitative social order to the exact extent that said discourse promotes exploitation" (Gilyard 49). These are hard words to hear because, in my experience, teachers are not intentionally oppressing students but the evidence is that generally teachers do avoid dealing with race in their classrooms to ill effect.

Together Learning How to Talk About Race

Instructors can and do learn what to do and not do in the race talk that commonly emerges in the classroom, whether or not it is part of the structured curriculum. As I shared with the conference participants, given the opportunity for a small but extended (6-week) experience in readings, dialogue, and other hands-on activities, the ten faculty and staff members of a study group at a small, liberal arts university in southwest PA achieved both cognitive and emotional outcomes from the experience. The group was comprised of five African Americans and five White people, four of whom were faculty and six were staff members, including Barbara Johnson (African American), the university's director of student diversity, and myself (White), faculty, who co-facilitated. All were female in their fifties and early sixties and had worked at the university from three to more than 16 years. Pre- and post-study group self-report surveys indicated the following changes:

- They improved their ability to express themselves when discussing sensitive issues.
- They felt more comfortable asking people different from themselves about their perspectives.
- They worried less about offending people from other groups when they disagree.
- They were more willing to learn about other groups different from their own.
- They felt the need to help different groups learn from each other.
- They felt less frustrated in interactions with people from other identity groups.
- They had a greater understanding and awareness of stereotypes.
- They were more empathetic.
- They were less despairing about inequity although simultaneously angrier about it.
- They felt less certain that conflict makes people fearful although they are still uncertain that it can enrich a discussion.
- They felt more certain that talking about conflicts helps clarify misunderstandings that groups have about each other.
- They believed conflict could have a positive impact on others and positive consequences overall, resulting in a healthy impact on democracy.
- They felt much more able to help people use conflict constructively.
- They felt that they learned more about themselves in conflict situations, including that they tend to clam up and freeze in the face of strong emotions.

- They were more confident that they can recognize and challenge their own biases, avoid language with negative stereotypes, and reinforce others for behaviors that support cultural diversity.
- They remain unsure they can challenge others' derogatory comments yet.
- They are confident they can make efforts to educate themselves about other groups, get to know others from other groups, join a community organization that promotes diversity, get together with others to challenge discrimination, and participate in a coalition to address social issues.

In addition, some respondents chose to write comments about the study group experience. One participant concluded, "I have an increased awareness about the people in the world around me, and a desire to better understand my fellow human beings. I especially enjoyed the listening exercises and hope to practice listening more effectively." Another wrote, "I learned in order for our society to grow and for our people to [be valued] equally, I must take on the challenge to become educated about different groups, educate others, which means I may have to confront conflict, motivate myself to engage in different diversity groups and stay persistent at this and hopefully I will set an example for all to see." Another participant realized "all groups who aren't 'privileged' receive hurtful messages—some are obvious while others aren't as apparent [and] cause lasting damage to one's self-esteem." Finally, one study group member commented, "I learned again the power of simple, honest conversation." Overall, the surveys indicated that members of the study group now knew people who were different from themselves on a deeper level than they had before.

In other words, teachers need and welcome professional development in intergroup communication competency. It is advisable and defensible to request such meaningful professional development opportunities, like attendance at the Intergroup Dialogue Institute at the University of Michigan or inviting a consultant or other speakers to help the campus assess its institutional barriers to such a campus movement.

But I suggest also that teachers not wait for the institutional ocean liner to turn and head for the waters of diversity education. Even a little tug boat can have an impact. But teachers cannot wait to start their own work until the institution begins its work. This book is meant to empower teachers sufficiently so that they can personally get started on the work of using compassionate listening with critical challenge.

Our society is depending upon teachers to develop racial competency so that they can interrupt racism when and where needed as well as to retrain students to critically assess situations and to respond with intelligence and compassion. Being on the "front lines" in the classroom and campus spaces, teachers are an appropriate and necessary source of leadership to fix daily microaggressions (our own and others') as they occur. As many scholars attest, teachers are content and process experts, but they are also natural leaders who can repair the inadequacies of curriculum and teacher preparation that frame students of color as deficient (Coburn et al.; Evans; Ladson-Billings). Institutions must recognize and provide time and space for teachers to exercise this expertise on behalf of the university community.

Moreover, the colleges and universities must scrutinize the discriminatory policies and practices of our schools, both deliberate and defacto, which trap us all in useless and damaging reiteration and reinforcement of racism and White supremacy. For example, programs that provide "remediation" or other support for students identified as "high risk" have strong racial biases and often house racist practices, frequently with the best of intentions, but are important teaching sites and deserve critical reassessment and revision (Lamos 69–71). In another instance, service-learning programs often unintentionally reify stereotypical attitudes about race, class, and social responsibility when not structured to build critical awareness and intergroup competency (Green; Herzberg). Further, most college faculty are White, notes Audrey Williams June in an article on the "invisible labor" and "cultural taxation" paid by faculty of color as mentors to high numbers of students of color. Because most faculty are White, many college curricula and cultures house and sustain a White dominant narrative. I offer for just a beginning list of examples, Victor Villanueva's characterization of representation by people of color in the professional English journals at "infinitesimal" (Villanueva 836) as well as his own personal account of microaggressions against him and his graduate students in that same chapter of his seminal reader, *Cross-Talk in Theory*.

Add to that the highly charged March 2019 national conversation on the Writing Program Administrators List-serve sparked by a racist post amidst the discussion about rhetorician Asao Inoue's keynote speech at the 2019 Conference on College Composition and Communication. Inoue's call to English instructors to undo the White Supremacy inherent in the field's assessment standards and to make room for different voices unleashed a debate about the primacy and morality of the entire discipline of English, and the near collapse of the long-running list-serve as it was conceived and managed. The outrage, confusion, and upheaval that marked the instructors' reactions testified to their need for space, time, and support in considering views and approaches behind the dominant White narrative (Flaherty). It vividly demonstrated some people's "White fragility" (DiAngelo) and near-total inability to (1) recognize their own culpability in maintaining White privilege and racism in spite of their best intentions, and (2) imagine the kinds of curricular and pedagogical changes needed to function in a diverse society with awareness and integrity. Frankly, when faced with racial conflict, teachers, including myself, don't know how to respond well to each other or their students.

Teachers are daily swimming in a sea of racism that threatens to drown them and the work they hope to do. They must find ways to speak up, to feel supported in speaking up, to support each other, or the boat will overturn and their hard work and hopes all wash down the drain. In considering the importance of Whites finding their anti-racist voices in this system, Johnson imagines a scene in which

> … a gang of White men are beating a person of color in broad daylight on a city street. I'm standing in a crowd of White people who are watching. We aren't hurting anyone. We feel no ill will toward the man being beaten and may feel sorry for him. We aren't cheering the attackers on or showing any outward signs of approval. We're just standing in silence, "minding our own business." And then one of the men stops, looks up, and says, his eyes panning across our faces, "We appreciate your support. We couldn't do this without you."(Johnson 106)

Johnson goes on to explain that it is the "passive oppression" of White people that sustains racism in our society because White people generally fail to act against racism or to speak up when needed. Doing nothing to interrupt racism allows it to continue and even strengthens it.

The intent, the goal of this book is to help teachers and institutions overcome the pervasive fear of talking about racism and feel capable of breaking the silence around racism and its power over lives of all colors. Using *compassionate listening* coupled with questions or comments that provide a *critical challenge* to false assumptions and other prejudice, teachers will know what to say and do when faced with race talk in their classes or meetings or research. Teachers need to find their voices, personally and institutionally, so that they can upset the current balance that disadvantages so many. It is by learning to recognize and name the underpinnings of race talk that they can de-fang it, that they can defuse their own shock, confusion, or fear enough to speak out in ways that deconstruct the power of racist language and ideas and to show the students how to do the same. Schools, colleges and universities must step up to support teachers in their personal journeys and professional readiness to undertake, even step by step, the curricular and policy revision needed for more humane, more effective, more equitable teaching, learning, and living. The next chapter's story of the research methods and the field's trailblazers in this effort offer much insight and hope that the tremendous task of anti-racist reform is not only possible but within the reach of every teacher, and every school or college.

Works Cited

Adams, Maurianne et al. *Teaching for Diversity and Social Justice*. 2nd edition. Routledge, 2007.

Baxter Magolda, Marcia B. and Patricia M. King. *Learning Partnerships: Theory and Models of Practice to Educate for Self-Authorship*. Stylus, 2004.

Chesler, Mark. *The Role of Facilitators*. Handout, The Program on Intergroup Relations, The University of Michigan, 2011.

Coburn, Cynthia E. et al. "Evidence, Interpretation, and Persuasion: Instructional Decision Making at the District Central Office." *Teacher's College Record*, vol. 111, no. 4, 2009, pp. 1115–1161.

DiAngelo, Robin. *White Fragility*. Beacon Press, 2018.

Evans, Andrea E. "School Leaders and Their Sensemaking About Race and Demographic Change." *Educational Administration Quarterly*, vol. 43, 2007, pp. 159–188, http://eaq.sagepub.com/cgi/content/abstract/43/2/159.

Feagin, Joe R. *The White Racial Frame: Centuries of Racial Framing and Counter-Framing*. Routledge, 2010.

Flaherty, Colleen. "Racist Writing Instructor's Listserv Post Prompts Debate About Future of the Field and How Scholars Communicate." *Inside Higher Ed*, Inside Higher Ed, 28 March 2019.

Gilyard, Keith. "Higher Learning: Composition's Racialized Reflection." *Race, Rhetoric, and Composition*, edited by Keith Gilyard. Boynton/Cook Publishers, 1999, pp. 44–52. *Crosscurrents*, Charles I. Schuster.

Goodburn, Amy. "Racing (Erasing) White Privilege in Teacher/Research Writing About Race." *Race, Rhetoric and Composition*, edited by Keith Gilyard. Boynton/Cook Publishers, 1999, pp. 67–86. *Cross Currents*, Charles I. Schuster.

Green, Ann E. "Difficult Stories: Service-Learning, Race, Class and Whiteness." *College Composition and Communication*, vol. 55, no. 2, 2003, pp. 276–301.

Gurin, Patricia. "The Expert Report of Patricia Gurin." University of Michigan, 2003. http://www.vpcomm.umich.edu/admissions/legal/expert/gurintoc.html, 11 October 2003.

Herzberg, Bruce. "Community Service and Critical Teaching." *Writing the Community: Concepts and Models for Service Learning in Composition*, edited by Linda Adler-Kassner, Robert Crooks, and Ann Watters. American Association for Higher Education in cooperation with the National Council of Teachers of English, 1997, pp. 57–70. *Service-Learning in the Disciplines*, Edward Zlotkowski.

Houts Picca, Leslie and Joe R. Feagin. *Two-Faced Racism: Whites in the Backstage and the Frontstage*. Routledge, 2007.

Johnson, Allan G. *Privilege, Power, and Difference*. 2nd edition. McGraw-Hill, 2006.

Knott, Katherine. "What It's Like to Be Named to a Watch List of 'Anti-American' Professors." *The Chronicle of Higher Education*, The Chronicle of Higher Education, 23 November 2016.

Kovaleski, Serge F. et al. "An Alt-Right Makeover Shrouds Swastikas." *The New York Times*, National edition, vol. CLXVI.57433, The New York Times Company, 11 December 2016.

Kuh, George, Thomas F. Nelson Laird, Paul d. Umbach. "Aligning Faculty Activities & Student Behavior: Realizing the Promise of Greater Expectations." *Liberal Education*, vol. 90, no. 4, 2004, pp. 24–31, Academic Search Elite/ERIC.

Ladson-Billings, Gloria. "Toward a Theory of Culturally Relevant Pedagogy." *American Educational Research Journal*, vol. 32, no. 3, 1995, pp. 465–491, JSTOR.

Lamos, Steve. "Language, Literacy, and the Institutional Dynamics of Racism: Late-1960s Writing Instruction for 'High-Risk' African American Undergraduate Students at One Predominantly White University." *College Composition and Communication*, vol. 60, no. 1, 2008, pp. 46–81.

Maxwell, Kelly E. et al. *Facilitating Intergroup Dialogues: Bridging Differences, Catalyzing Change*. Stylus Publishing, LLC, 2011.

McIntyre, Alice. *Making Meaning of Whiteness: Exploring Racial Identity with White Teachers*. State University of New York Press, 1997.

Pimentel, Octavio. "Invitation to a Too-Long Postponed Conversation: Race and Composition." *Reflections: Public Rhetoric, Civic Writing, and Service Learning*, vol. 12, no. 2, 2013, pp. 90–109.

Potok, Mark. "The Beast Reawakens." Southern Poverty Law Center https://www.splcenter.org/fighting-hate/intelligence-report/2016/beast-reawakens. Accessed 10 December 2016.

Ratcliffe, Krista. *Rhetorical Listening: Identification, Gender, Whiteness*. Southern Illinois University Press, 2005. *Studies in Rhetorics and Feminisms*, Shirley Glenn and Shirley Wilson Logan.

Strauss, Valerie. "A Twist on Controversial 'Professor Watchlist': Notre Dame Academics Want Their Names Added." *The Washington Post*, The Washington Post, 8 December 2016, Answer Sheet.

Sue, Derald Wing. *Race Talk and the Conspiracy of Silence*. John Wiley & Sons, Inc., 2015.

Tatum, Beverly Daniel. *"Why Are All the Black Kids Sitting Together in the Cafeteria?" And Other Conversations About Race*. Basic Books, 2003.

The Program on Intergroup Relations. "*Useful Questions for Dialogue Facilitation*." Handout, University of Michigan, 2006.

Trainor, Jennifer Seibel. *Rethinking Racism: Emotion, Persuasion, and Literacy Education in an All-White High School.* Southern Illinois University Press, 2008.

TuSmith, Bonnie. "Out on a Limb: Race and the Evaluation of Frontline Teaching." *Race in the College Classroom: Pedagogy and Politics*, edited by Bonnie TuSmith and Maureen T. Reddy. Rutgers University Press, 2002, pp. 112–125.

Villanueva, Victor. "On the Rhetoric and Precedents of Racism." *Cross-Talk in Comp Theory: A Reader*, edited by Victor Villanueva, 2nd edition. National Council of Teachers of English, 2003, pp. 829–845.

Villanueva, Victor and Robert Eddy. *A Language & Power Reader: Representations of Race in a "Post-Racist" Era*. Utah University Press, 2014.

Zuniga, Ximena et al. "Intergroup Dialogue in Higher Education: Meaningful Learning About Social Justice." *Jossey-Bass Higher and Adult Education Series*, edited by Kelly Ward and Lisa E. Wolf-Wendel, vol. 32, no. 4, Report, Association for the Study of Higher Education, Winter 2007.

· 2 ·

METHODOLOGY AND LITERATURE: HOW DID WE GET TO THIS PLACE AND TIME?

This book is the story of four students who found themselves in a first-year college composition course where they were forced to confront race. It's also the story of their struggle with that focus, how it looked to them at the time, just after they'd finished the course, as well as how they felt it had affected them four years later as they graduated from the college, a small, Catholic, predominantly female liberal arts institution in a mid-sized rust-belt city. This book is deliberately not a comprehensive study of a large group. Focusing small, this story is made easier to hear and think about *because* it is the story of only four students; you will get to know them each and be able to look more closely and listen more intently for things unsaid as well as those actually spoken in the interviews.

Most likely, you will recognize these particular young people are typical of many first-year students in their sincere desire to do well, to "get it right," to earn a good grade and perhaps the teacher's respect for their skill and ambitions. At the same time and again quite typically, they were a little unsure that they could measure up, a little nervous that perhaps their previous learning in English composition might have some gaps. What is not typical of most first-year college classes is that their insecurity pretty quickly turned to curiosity, discomfort, and in some cases, near-terror when they realized that we were going to talk and write about race and racism for the entire semester.

My intent had been to challenge them, engage them fully in their topics so that they would be drawn, perhaps provoked, into deeper thinking about adult life in our society. In previous single-shot assignments, they had responded pretty energetically to writing and thinking about race, so the topic seemed promising and I decided to extend it to a full semester, as I detail in the next section. But I got a little more than I had bargained for, which raised many challenges and questions for me then. I later realized their reactions had implications for all of us who choose to employ critical pedagogy in the college classroom. Critical pedagogy, a student-centered approach also known as liberatory pedagogy, grows out of the 1970s work of social justice educators, like Paolo Freire, Ira Shor, and Henry Giroux. It focuses on cultural critique and the problematization of the students' own experience with institutionalized inequity using dialogue towards social justice action. It fits easily into English studies and composition because of the discipline's interdisciplinary nature. Compositionist Ann George argues that Freirean theory has a strong relationship to English as a field, "Because language and thought are inextricably linked, language instruction becomes a key site where dominant ideology is reproduced—or disrupted" (94). Thus, an English course that uses critical pedagogy "aims to help students develop the tools that will enable them to challenge this inequality," employing "its usually explicit commitment to education for citizenship" (George 92–93). The plan, then, was to teach writing in the context of social justice, specifically anti-racism.

As in many classes, though, these students were not necessarily expecting either critical pedagogy or anti-racism in a writing class. Their reactions and thoughts about the course experiences ran the gamut, as described later, providing a richly nuanced snapshot of all the phases of the continuum I came to learn was racial identity development. The trick—the conundrum—for teachers, as well as their colleges and universities, is to figure out how to respond to the breadth and depth of student responses while managing their own (lack of) racially diverse experience and emotional triggers.

I argue in this book that the key is to reframe the student's responses, to understand them as sincere efforts to make sense of their past education and experience in race while trying to still hold on to their treasured emotional investment in their past world and relationships with family, friends, neighbors, and community. As racist as the student responses might actually be, students and teachers need to own them, understand their sources, and forgive past words and actions, as well as and especially the lack of knowledge about each other across the color lines. Teachers need to find ways to educate themselves that are more meaningful and effective than the required or strongly suggested diversity workshop. We need to change what we know and how we know it to be able to help us understand ourselves, our speaking and writing, our concept of and interactions with other people different from ourselves, and to function with the compassion and responsibility that we hold as necessary for every fully educated individual and for a peaceful world.

The shift from talking simply about the students to talking about us in the previous paragraph is not a grammatical error or Freudian slip; it is intentional. This book is about student responses to race and racism as it emerges in class study but also about us, the teachers, including myself, who must be able to accurately and bravely name, appropriately reframe and redirect our students' as well as our own reactions with enlightened compassion and fuller, concrete information about living race in twenty-first century America.

The information we need is in these student interviews. The words of the students, set against and in the context of the vast literature on the history and current social realities of race, racism, white privilege, identity, and resistance, yield a useful narrative of how we do race today, in our classrooms and communities, and what directions we can take to enact greater justice for us all.

To that end, this chapter will provide a description of the course that is the basis of this research, as well as an introduction to the theoretical underpinnings of the analysis of each of the student interviews.

Some Background: What We Did in the Class and How It Felt

The interviews upon which this work is based first occurred in January 2007, after their fall course finished, and then at various times in the 2009–2010 school year, their senior year, with one occurring in 2011. In the intervening years since these interviews, the hundreds of students who been in similar iterations of this course with me have reacted to the course and responded in similar ways, so I believe they are fairly representative of students in courses like this one. Specifically, in the two Fall 2006 sections I was teaching, the course was the required one-semester composition course, using a typical English department syllabus that was process-oriented and text-directed but open-ended in the teacher's choice of themes for specific assignments. The text was organized around the modes of discourse (personal, information, evaluation, persuasion, problem analysis essays). I tied each essay to race in some way in order to help students move from novice writer to expert writer who can sustain deeper reflection and critical thinking on a topic. This approach was a conscious effort to compensate for a core curriculum that required only a single-semester college writing experience.

In my sections, the students wrote about some aspect of the topic of race for the entire semester so that we could move past the basics of race and write with greater knowledge and authority. I was trying to simulate in one semester the depth and confidence that the Harvard Study of Writing documented among writers who returned to the same topic repeatedly over the duration of their college careers (Sommers and Saltz). Thus, I constructed each essay assignment as a broadly framed task related to racial identity, privilege, Whiteness, or racial discrimination: a time when you felt different, a race-related topic a family member needs to understand, whether or not the film we watched actually helps viewers learn about race, and how racism displays in their major or career field.

We used Beverly Daniel Tatum's popular *"Why Are All the Black Kids Sitting Together in the Cafeteria?" And Other Conversations About Race* as our primary text. As part of our prewriting activity, students tried to locate themselves on psychologist Janet Helms' seminal scale of White racial identity development. In the early 1990s, Helm explained in psycho-social terms how Blacks and Whites grew to understand their behaviors as raced people, progressing from responses to first contact with someone racially different, through positive integration of their respective identities. In between were many uncomfortable and confusing phases that Helms's research indicates not everyone successfully traverses, stages with names like disintegration, reintegration, pseudo-independence, immersion/emersion, and autonomy (Helms "Black"). Students found it informative and empowering, though, to consider the kinds of personal changes they could possible make.

Students also tested Peggy McIntosh's famous knapsack list of White privileges . We watched the documentary series *Race: The Power of an Illusion* (Adelman), *Remember the Titans* (Yakin), *Freedom Writers* (LaGravanese), and later *Precious* (Daniels) and *Crash* (Haggis), analyzing characters' behaviors (and their own) in terms of its sources in childhood upbringing and/or the pressures of their racist teachers, parents, and community leaders.

But as engaged as the students were, they struggled with the curriculum. Their shallow, forgotten, or non-existent background in the history of slavery, Jim Crow, the Civil Rights Movement, and important figures beyond Dr. Martin Luther King often handicapped their understanding of current events and issues, leaving their critical thinking weak and their arguments underdeveloped, insensitive or illogical. Most had very little experience with anyone different from themselves although they almost all claimed to once have had a close friend who was Black. They didn't see any reason to talk about race because that was a problem for their parents and grandparents, not their generation. Yet when they tried to discuss some aspect of race, they vacillated between insensitivity, even outright racism, and overwhelmed silence.

The mood of the class was volatile, moving from confusion and anger to the heartwarming personal story or insight, then back again to pain and resistance, often within the space of minutes. It was uncomfortable, an uphill battle every day, and far more demanding of us all, myself included, than we were used to. So, they pushed back. Despite my efforts to connect it all to identity, voice, argument, and logic, students objected, "This is isn't writing! Why can't we write about what we want?"

Not wanting to believe they were choosing to stay uninformed, intentionally racist, or entirely without compassion, I heard their message as, "Still not enough persuasive facts!" So I gathered more sociological and psychological data. We talked about personal, internalized, and institutional racism with help from Tolerance.org, the Southern Poverty Law Center, Tatum, Feagin, and more. I thought this factual information was the knowledge that would surely persuade my students to see the world and others differently.

But the students didn't see it that way. They were angry at me, Tatum and others for, in their views, accusing them, their families, and friends of being racists. They separated into different camps—the visibly angry, the angry below the surface, and those that just walked away, with a smattering of students who either became passionately anti-racist or felt confirmed in their anti-racism. No one in the literature seemed to know how to deal with these reactions, other than to plow ahead. Moreover, I felt very susceptible to the accusations that I was inappropriately bringing politics into the classroom (Durst, Hairston).

I knew in my gut that there had to be more to this analysis, but both my students and I seemed to be struggling to breathe in the face of a firehose of emotion opened on us at every turn in the curriculum. They were trying to keep a relentlessly positive outlook in the face of poverty, racism, and other suffering, always finding an exception to the facts, a flower pushing up through the cracked concrete. On many days, the task to find some common ground seemed overwhelming, both to them and to me.

As the class progressed, I realized that my students were saying that my Cartesian separation of "the facts" from the emotions of race study was leaving them high and dry. They were caught in an unnamed struggle to hold on to their families, their memories, their idea of their teachers, churches, coaches, political leaders, and other institutional/cultural connections as basically good people in the face of evidence that they had participated in the maintenance of racism in our society.

This judgment didn't sit well with the students, but there didn't seem any way out for them and they faced an impossible choice. To accept that racism and discrimination still happened today was to abandon their belief that they and theirs were still good people. They would be in a new lonely space, having to dispute the jokes, the stereotypes, their privilege, which they could hardly believe they really had. None of this hardship felt like privilege. The other choice was to somehow block out what they now knew and return to their old lack of awareness and live with the guilt. The cognitive dissonance was palpable at times in our classroom. I wasn't sure how to go on in some useful, meaningful way.

How This Book Developed: The Methodology of This Research Project

After a few years of teaching a racially themed first-year writing, I was seeking some verification that an anti-racist curriculum was an effective pedagogy for a first-year composition course. From a critical pedagogy perspective, I wanted to document how the curriculum was affecting their thinking on and about race in our society. From a composition perspective, I wanted to validate my observations that student essays were consistently more complex than when I'd used other approaches, and students seemed much more engaged in and connected with their writing. Besides that, class discussion had generally shifted from concerns about grammar and essay length to rhetorical concerns about their audience and support of their arguments. This shift seemed good but I wanted some empirical evidence to back my anecdotes. Thus, this research project was born.

For this study, using an IRB-approved methodology, I recruited students from the two classes I was teaching (32 total enrollment), submitting thirteen of their names blindly to a third party, emphasizing no connection to their grades, and conducting the actual research after their semester grades had been submitted. The analysis of the thirteen essays became the bulk of my dissertation, *The Effects of Race-Themed Composition Instruction on Student Writing*. One of the dissertation chapters focused on interviews with five apparently White students, who had volunteered for that in addition to sharing their essays. After interviewing all five women, I found one White student's interview unusable because her answers were so short and unrevealing, perhaps due to White fragility (DiAngelo), discussed later. One of the two African American young women in the class had also volunteered but dropped out before the interviews, apparently due to time constraints. All were 18 years old. All were female because the university was small and predominantly female.

What I came to understand later was that one of the remaining "White" students actually identified as Middle Eastern, as well as White, a significant point of confusion for all of us as I will discuss a little later. So, in essence, this project was a convenience sample of four White women participants and one Middle Eastern, self-selected for reasons I only briefly examined and, as such, the study makes no claims to being a comprehensive analysis of race in the classroom.

In an initial stage of this project, I analyzed two writing samples from a much broader group of students, including the interview participants, one early in the semester and one later, to determine if they were learning to write competently within the racially themed format of the class. I holistically scored the samples to gauge the level of critical thinking among other features, using Bloom's taxonomy and my university's departmental rubric, thinking that at some point I might compare them to students in a similar but non-racially themed class. Because no one else in the department was teaching or grading this way, I did not have a second scorer. Still, the project was a start in "proving" to colleagues and myself that this pedagogy was a valid approach to teaching writing.

In time, my hubris quieted, I realized that I wasn't "proving" anything, and that the most valuable piece of this project was not captured in the writing samples but in the interviews. They were an opportunity to hear the voices of some of the students, to understand how they experienced the course and its artificially inseminated encounter with racism.

The interviews were private sessions, conducted in my office, using a digital voice recorder while I took notes. I used open-ended questions that, in the first year, focused on their current awareness of and understanding of their own racial identity and how that was impacted by the experience of the course, particularly their writing, as well as how the writing impacted their learning about race and racism. In the senior year, the questions focused on their racial awareness and identity growth since the class, the impact of other course learning and lived experience in the dorms, at work, in their neighborhoods, and with other students from other colleges and universities.

I first analyzed the interviews for indications of racial identity stage markers, based on the descriptions of stages of racial identity development from Janet Helms and Beverly Daniel Tatum. Later, other scholars became relevant in the study of individual interviews, including Marcia Baxter Magolda's and Patricia King's work on college student self-authorship that describes the Venn-diagram nexus of cognitive maturity with an integrated identity and mature relationships to produce effective citizenship as a central outcome (Baxter Magolda and King 7). I also found insight in Joe Feagin's White racial frame and his analysis with Leslie Houts Picca of thousands of college students' racial event diaries that flesh out how virulent racism is still in "backstage" single-race settings (Houts Picca and Feagin).

Similarly, Tatum's explication of both Black and White young people's racial identity development (52–74, 93–113), Derald Wing Sue's qualitative analysis of "race talk," Krista Ratcliffe's theorization of student resistances to race talk (133–141), and Jennifer Seibel Trainor's rich narrative of high school students caught between critical racism and the dominant positive citizenship narrative (*Rethinking Racism*) all enriched my understanding of my students' struggles.

Each interview included in this book elucidates the reactions, thinking, fears and hopes of a student who comes from a unique social identity influenced by her own personality, family, friends, school, church, neighborhood, city or suburb and sees the world from her individual perspective. While they have similarities, each provides a different picture of a particular kind of struggle with the racism and its role in shaping that person's understanding of her past, present, and future. Ultimately, each student responds a little (sometimes a lot) differently, in some predictable but at other times shocking ways, making clear that they—and we—are anything but post-racial and that we all still have much work to do.

Helpful Context: Racial Identity Development, Resistance, and Emotion

An understanding of the students in this book as well as students and teachers familiar to readers relies on grasping the process and significance for people in American society of the development of racial identity. Like most human development, racial identity is ripe with opportunity and fraught with difficulty; this work can feel out-of-control, scary, guilt-producing, painful. Without information about privilege and oppression, strategies to help process it productively, and support from colleagues and/or institutions, teachers understandably avoid the issues, communicating to students, just as the rest of society does, that race is an untouchable, unmanageable topic too dangerous for good people to discuss. People of all colors are silenced into secret suspicions that differences between us position some of us to be less than others. People need information, skills in critical analysis and dialogue, and institutional structures that support courageous ventures into the borderlands between racial identities.

I only gradually realized the need for more race talk, with help mostly from my friends at the YWCA, (formerly known as the Young Women's Christian Association), whose mission is "The empowerment of women and the elimination of racism," and eventually from colleagues whose fields touched on race. They cheered me on, telling me this work was important, but had few concrete suggestions for how to apply the theory in my first-year writing classes beyond a quick workshop. Students were ready for more depth and agility in their critical thinking about content but also about themselves and each other. Learning to communicate about race, a topic both personal and public, could be a powerfully apt vehicle for improving thinking and writing. Finding a pathway to deeper learning about their own racial identity could open doors, build bridges, and break down walls between them and a bigger world. Otherwise, they would retreat to re-segregation, settling for much less than their rhetorical and psychological/emotional potential and a much narrower experience of friends, family, work, neighborhood, life. I sought out other experts in the literature who knew more about the possible pathways. The following will be a quick summary of some of my intellectual mentors, many of whom will figure prominently in the analysis of the student interviews in subsequent chapters, as well as suggestions in the end.

Beverly Daniel Tatum gently but frankly taught me about racial social norms, privilege, and how racial awareness develops across the age cycle for people who are Black, other non-dominant groups, and White. Her book "*Why Are All the Black Kids Sitting Together in the Cafeteria?" And Other Conversations About Race* helped me and the students understand that children develop a social identity right from the start, recognizing racial difference as young as three years of age (Tatum 32) and absorbing the dominant (White) social norms about their group and others. As I reference often in this book, Tatum uses the apt metaphor of the "smog" of racism that infects and permeates our society; with welcome forgiveness she explains that none of us can avoid breathing it and so we are all affected by it and absorb it whether or not we intend it (Tatum 6).

As Tatum notes, the most common organizing metaphor in racial identity development theory is that people experience stages of awareness of race, both their own and others.' Psychologist Janet Helms is generally credited as among the first to systematize this psychological theory related to Whites, building on the 1970s work of Cross and others (Helms "Introduction" 6). Because racial identity is experienced differently in a racialized society, there are different "stages" of racial identity development for Blacks and Whites. My book focuses largely on White racial identity development because the majority of the students studied were White. According to Helms, the stages for White students in the development of a positive White identity are: (1) contact, (2) disintegration, (3) re-integration, (4) pseudo-independence (5) immersion/emersion, (5), and autonomy (Helms "Toward" 49–66). Each of these stages will be further described and the stage theory critiqued in later chapters. I mention them here to provide context for the subsequent discussion of manifestations of the contact and disintegration stages that dominate racial interaction in U.S. society, even as we pass the *sesquicentennial* of the 1863 Emancipation Proclamation ending slavery in this country.

Tatum's recasting of Janet Helms's stages of racial identity development redeemed that groundbreaking work from objections by some scholars that stage theory oversimplifies the process because development is not linear as the stages imply. Tatum made clear that real people make their way through racial identity growth in spirals, cycling sometimes forward, sometimes backward again rather than in a straight linear march.

Tatum's work struck me as intellectually rich and gave the students accessible personalized markers of experience that buoyed much discussion and insight. But as predominantly White students in the "contact" and "disintegration" stages, they struggled mightily with the hard realities of White privilege. They'd say, What do you mean "privilege?" I've worked hard and my parents have worked hard. We are not rich! And then we'd slide into angry stories of someone who knew someone who … got a job or a scholarship because she was Black … lived in Section 8 (subsidized) housing but drove a big, fancy car … kept having babies by different men so she could collect welfare and watch her TV soaps … was a third-generation welfare family … got her nails done and spent hundreds of dollars each month at the beauty parlor … couldn't be bothered with proper English but still got passed in school and then got a free ride to college and maybe a big-salary sports career … and on and on. Often students blamed Tatum for their sense of cognitive dissonance, but she also helped many see with different eyes.

Krista Ratcliffe, another mentor of mine, provides a precise description of a range of student resistances to social critique and the study of race and difference helped me name their behaviors for the first time (138–139). I had personally witnessed everything in her catalogue—denial, dismissal, indifferent compliance, defensiveness, overidentification, nonproductive guilt, adherence to gender- and/or color-blindness, and speaking block or writing block. I could put students' names to these resistance scenarios.

I also got help from Marlia Banning, who provided a helpful Marxist perspective . She argued that student resistance and resentment are righteous but displaced from its true cause: the powers that keep institutional racism alive in our society, making us all victims of distrust and disinformation on a daily basis.

In response to the Banning article in the *Journal of Advanced Composition (JAC)*, Jennifer Seibol Trainer reiterated what eventually became her trademark thesis, that the highly emotioned "good citizens" training in the school system misleads students in their understanding of racism and ultimately causes their resentment (Trainor "From Identity"). An outgrowth of suburban segregation, the curriculum teaches that good people are color blind, work hard in spite of obstacles, and keep a relentlessly positive outlook in the face of poverty, racism, and other suffering. Students are not taught a more complex critical understanding of the institutional flaws of social systems. Trainor argues that people don't learn what to do with the cognitive dissonance that arises from the clash of oversimplified civic pride lessons and the realities of negative experiences that grow out of racism (*Rethinking Racism*). Again, my students looked and sounded like those that Trainor studied—shocked, angry, confused, hurt.

As the following interviews show, their anger was very real and came from deep personal spaces. They were very vulnerable to an oral tradition pervasive in their lives of Black deficit and White normativity and misunderstood or didn't know the context for much of what they had actually observed. The emotions were raw and the myths and prejudice felt factual to them. As we read Tatum's book together, they interpreted her frank but generous room-for-all logic as stinging accusation that they were White and White people are in the wrong. The emotional stranglehold on beliefs they had always held far outweighed anything either Tatum or I had to say. I finally understood that facts, even gently couched facts, were not enough to make any headway with them.

Socialization, Aversive Racism and Their Cost to All

I hadn't fully realized the power of students' homes, communities, and other external influences. Harro points out that our socialization to our identities begins at birth or some say before then to assigned "values, roles, rules, models of ways to be, sources of dreams" (16), which are introduced and reinforced by family, school, church, media and other institutions, and other agents of cultural transmission. The clash between that socialization and our observations and experiences of difference in the world often produce results that are disconcerting, limiting and often disempowering. Harro's "cycle of socialization" describes a pivotal moment of negative results at the bottom of the cycle: "dissonance, silence, anger, dehumanization, guilt, collusion, ignorance, self-hatred, stress, lack of reality, horizontal violence, inconsistency, violence, crime, [and] internalization of patterns of power" (16). The discomfort of these results leads individuals to a climactic decision point to either change or actively commit to holding firm in the present position.

My students seemed to be at this decision point by the end of the class, as the interviews demonstrate, leaving some of them with a clear sense of direction (into future change or a return to the past) and some in a painful status quo limbo, avoiding any disturbance of their fragile equilibrium. But as helpful as the theoretical cycle was and is, again I was left with questions. What makes the difference in which direction a student chooses? Without getting Cartesian again, how much is related to empirical thought and how much to emotion? What can a teacher access? How can teachers recognize and intervene in students' mental models?

Seeing the students' response in and to the class as part of their developmental journey clarifies the issues in several ways. Obviously, college students bring their early social identity work with them to the classroom. They are not yet finished adults. On our campuses, they continue their development towards self-authorship, which rests, according to Marcia Baxter Magolda and Patricia King, on the interactions of integrated identity, cognitive maturity, and mature relationships, all leading to effective citizenship. Self-authorship requires an epistemological foundation (knowledge), and intrapersonal foundation (identity), and an interpersonal foundation (relationships, community responsibility) (Baxter Magolda and King 7–8). If students are lucky, their schooling and young adult experiences challenge their earlier socialization, particularly their racial identity, so that they can resolve the disconnects and hateful results of living in a racialized society.

To students and the teachers trying to assist them, hope in a resolution or a place beyond their cognitive dissonance, discomfort, and disillusion sometimes seems a little too ethereal to help in moments of difficulty or even despair. My students often reached a point, after about five weeks of study of race and writing, often in their first college semester, where they were overwhelmed with the immensity of the problems of the world, race being only one of them. Hope is too amorphous at that point, too far a reach.

After all, they have seen few models of living an integrated life. In testimony to the Supreme Court on behalf of the University of Michigan's case for race-conscious admissions, historian Thomas Sugrue explains that these students (and their teachers) have lived, attended school, worshipped, and socialized in "separate worlds" (Sugrue) and generally have not really known anyone different from themselves before coming to college. The confusion of "American" values of freedom, liberty and individualism with the racism upon which our economy and political system are built (Feagin *Racist America*) leads White people to believe that talking about race at all is somehow reifying racism and contributing to the problem (King 133). In an article on affirmative action, Dovidio, Mann, and Gaertner provide one of the earliest references to the term "aversive racism" to describe "an attitudinal adaptation resulting from an assimilation of an egalitarian value system with prejudice and racist beliefs" (qtd. in Tatum 118). Such aversion accounts for White unwillingness to squarely face racial talk or action because Whites have been in charge (dominant) and so acknowledging racism's existence reflects badly on White performance and identity. White people who want to maintain their self-concept as just and unbiased need to actively avoid attributing any injustice to race to avoid accountability for it. This White avoidance of seeing race and racism, even as it stares people in the face, is the same as DiAngleo's "white fragility," as mentioned earlier.

The aversion to seeing race has racist negative effects because it denies responsibility for and the existence of conditions that privilege Whites over Blacks, Latino(as), Asians, Native Americans, and other people of color. Studies of college students indicate the complexity of the psychological maneuvering necessary to avoid seeing their privilege in order to shield their self-esteem. White students must find fault outside of themselves or the institution, that is in "Others" and/or see themselves as superior. So, "Black students were not rated as more lazy than Whites, but Whites were evaluated as more ambitious than Blacks," and identically qualified Black and White job candidates were rated positively, but White participants scored Black applicants "significantly less positively" than Whites (Tatum 119–120). This kind of doublespeak is the basis of the aversion that underlies continued stereotyping of Blacks, and continued residential segregation and employment discrimination, among other social deficits (Feagin *Racist America* 168,238; Sugrue). Aversive racism is, thus, both directly and indirectly a contributor to the experience of racism on campus.

On campuses and in the rest of society, modern racism that expresses itself in aversion is often hard to identify because, by definition, it is a form of psychological denial, a non-entity in the mind of the agent. King refers to this White lack of consciousness of an aversive stance as "dysconscious racism," that is,

> … an uncritical habit of mind (including perceptions, attitudes, assumptions, and beliefs) that justifies inequity and exploitation by accepting the existing order of things as given … Dysconscious racism is a form of racism that tacitly accepts dominant White norms and privileges. It is not the *absence* of consciousness (that is, not unconsciousness) but an *impaired* consciousness or distorted way of thinking about race as compared to, for example, critical consciousness. (135)

Without critical self reflection and critical analysis of society and its institutions, racism appears to be an external phenomenon, a large and uncontrollable mechanism beyond the reach or understanding of many White people who consider themselves anti-racist but generally powerless to effect change.

Because of teachers' vast sphere of influence on the coming generation, many researchers have studied this dysconsciousness-power dynamic among college students who intend to become teachers, noting their role in replicating and reinforcing the existing racialized and racist systems (Goodburn; King; McIntyre; Rosenberg; Trainor "Critical"). But any students, regardless of their field, who fail to critically reflect on their own role in perpetuating racism (Johnson and Staples) reinforce it by default (Bonilla-Silva; Chesler et al.; Fine). That is the key principle behind the multicultural education and critical pedagogy movements within education, to interrupt this causal link. That is also a crucial building block missing from much of current education; thus, institutional racism, including race problems in college, continue.

Other Complicating Mechanisms: Racelessness and Color Blindness

One aspect of 'dysconsciousness,' to extend King's term, is White people's lack of awareness that they are members of a racial group. Most White people define themselves by what they are *not:* not Black, not Native American, not Asian, not Hispanic or Latino (McIntyre 17). White is the default for "American" (Feagin *Racist America* 100; Pruitt 238). When circumstances pressure Whites to comment on themselves as raced, their response is often couched in "a model of White merit and superior morality … a range of sincere fictions about the White self, such as the images of White innocence and nobility …" (Feagin *Racist America* 110)

The result of seeing the self as privileged and somehow above race is that "the average White person does not see 'racism' or is less likely than ever to understand minorities' complaints" (Bonilla-Silva 283). In this model, White people, including students, remain unable to identify with the problems of others in any terms except their own, regardless of critical differences that point to institutional, rather than individual, responsibility for social problems and racial disparities (McIntyre 61). They largely do not see the catalogue of harms to people of color in our society that result directly from slavery and the racist assumptions built into our constitution, government, laws, policies, and practices from the founding days of our country (Zinn 97–99 Feagin, 2000 #120 9–67).They resist critique because, in their minds, the analysis of institutions that maintain racism feels like a personal attack (Rosenberg 259). They suffer misplaced and distracting guilt (King 136) and take refuge in color blindness (Bonilla-Silva; Rosenberg) and denial. To maintain their equilibrium and self-respect, they cannot see the need to change much in themselves or in society.

One thing White students don't understand is that, although they obviously do not suffer the consequences of racism in the same way or to the same degree as Black students, they do pay a price. Most of the negative consequences Whites suffer relate to a distorted view of reality and other people that causes problems for others and themselves. For example, Whites in denial live in continual fallacy, believing Whites and Blacks are equals but also, despite the contradiction, are "aware that being black in America involves major personal, family and economic costs" (Feagin *Racist America* 190). Similarly, some Whites will profess a love of parts of Black culture, such as jazz or rap, according to Ellis Cashmore, but "Aspects of the black experience can be integrated into the mainstream and … consumed without ever going near black people" (qtd. in Feagin *Racist America* 191). This kind of dishonesty takes a toll on self-knowledge, personal integrity and interpersonal relationships, particularly across racial lines.

Another cost to Whites is color-blindness, an aspect of the disintegration stage, that denies the differing social values attached to race. This form of denial vastly complicates and undercuts effective critical thinking and problem solving because color blindness also causes White people to not see the racial realities suffered daily by others who are not White. Teacher educator Pearl Rosenberg explains this dilemma in terms of the clinical condition of color blindness, describing its relationship to teacher education, as one particularly problematic field:

> Clinically color-blind people have to make guesses in order to fill in the gaps of information missing from their visual field. Their vision is imperfect, their experience incomplete. Thus, to be color blind is to suffer a loss. It makes no sense, therefore, to embrace color blindness as an ideal for the teacher in the classroom. And, yet, that is exactly where many of our preservice teachers begin. (257)

Of course, others in helping professions, the 'color-blind' doctor, lawyer, engineer, social worker, store clerk, waiter, librarian or any other person will also suffer this loss and may react innocently but inappropriately, perhaps damagingly, when responding to Black customers or clients, just as color-blind teachers might.

Whites who believe themselves superior to people of color will also pay the price of in trying to maintain a false identity, a stressful, uncomfortable process, explains Rosenberg: "[I]n such [racially hostile] environments, White students develop a profoundly false sense of superiority premised almost entirely on denigration which requires opposition to sustain the racial hierarchy. Opposition and denigration became a fix, a steroid to White identity" (249).

Lacking their own positive racial identity, poorly adjusted Whites will "expend considerable energy in screening out or denying potentially identity-shattering information" (Helms "Introduction" 87). They will often deteriorate to a "we-them" stance in which "zero-sum thinking" causes them to fear the loss of power or privilege if Blacks gain status of any kind (McIntyre 57). They will "distance" themselves from non-Whites in a variety of ways including flight from the cities, and pay the "price in terms of higher housing costs, long-distanced commuting, pollution from automobiles, and the social problems associated with metropolitan growth and central city decline" (Feagin *Racist America* 199).

Whites who are then forced by circumstances or experience to face the White role in producing and reproducing racial disparity and injustice often suffer guilt that can be quite paralyzing; some struggle with despair and self-loathing; others reject anti-racist involvement because it becomes too uncomfortable (Swim and Miller 501; Tatum 97). Many are left in fear of and alienation from Blacks and other non-White people (Feagin *Racist America* 200; McIntyre 136), having failed to integrate the new information about their racial identity. Needless to say, in a world that is growing "browner" by the day, such inability to live and work with non-White people will eventually become both a personal and professional detriment to the individual, family and associates.

Educational Implications

In additional testimony to the Supreme Court on behalf of the University of Michigan's case on race-conscious admissions, social psychologist Patricia Gurin addresses the compelling need for higher education to better integrate students' intergroup experiences and skills in order to enable students to ultimately participate effectively in work and civic life. Gurin maintains that the very life of democratic decision-making and other interaction between equals is at stake; to remain in the status quo is to lose touch with the possibility of living our nation's founding intentions and democratic ideals .

Without a school experience that includes deliberate attention to racial identity development, students (and teachers) find acceptance of the status quo inevitable. According to diversity educators Rita Hardiman and Bailey Jackson, people largely accept their status within a White-dominated society as either agents (members of the dominant group) or targets (members of the non-dominant group). On the part of White people, they have learned to passively accept as Truth the dominant beliefs that position White people as superior and people of color as inferior and at fault for their own oppression (Hardiman and Jackson 24–25).

As the interviews in this book show, college classes, like the one that motivated this study of a racially-themed writing class, hit students square in the face with radically different understandings of the world and their places in it. The course and college in general on even a mildly diverse campus sometimes provoke confrontations that create a painful negative encounter stage of racial identity for Black people and others of color while Whites experience a disintegration stage (Tatum 55, 96). As such, people of color may feel demeaned, oppressed, and helpless and White people may feel blamed and shamed. It's understandable then that if students are not confronted with course requirements to deal with racism, they tend to avoid the pain, disillusion, conflict, and sometimes guilt of engaging in racial identity growth.

But, as mentioned earlier, people need an encounter with alternative, non-dominant perspectives and a full critique of the White racial frame (Feagin). It is a necessary condition for individual growth, intellectual achievement, and social competence in a non-majority world. Allowing students (and teachers) to avoid this encounter is ultimately not helpful. The collateral damage of continuing to live blindly and aversively in this society is morally distasteful, degrading, unnecessarily guilt-producing and limiting of human potential. If nothing else, the inevitable demographic march to a "minority majority" by 2055 (Pew Research Center) will entrap all those who are unprepared in an apocalyptic lava slide toward seismic life change. So pragmatically speaking, if for no other reason, people—students and teachers—need to be ready to operate differently in a new world and learn to "see" race as it is in society, its differential impacts, and its call to personal, social, and institutional action.

My story of coming to new racial awareness and struggling to talk about it with my students is not extraordinary; in fact, that is the point. It is a very typical story, but one that, like race itself, does not get talked about very often in ways for classroom application. I believe that is because we teachers are raised and live in the same racialized world as everyone else. Whites live separately from people of color, go to different schools, worship in segregated groups, and learn the same fears and prejudiced frames (Sugrue). People share questionable jokes with friends and family in the backstage while striving for political correctness in the front stage (Houts Picca and Feagin). People all watch the same TV shows and movies that even with recent gains in diversity still symptomatically and institutionally struggle with representing non-White characters, understanding audiences of color, or casting and awarding actors beyond a narrow norm (Cieply; Dargis et al.). People vote for safer streets and erect drug-free zone signs that (unintentionally?) lead to racially disproportionate traffic stops, police use of excessive force against unarmed Black people, prisons bloated with too many Black and Brown faces, and a devastated Black community (Coates). People's lives, even for people are color, are conducted in a very White world, leaving them with little context or sometimes even awareness that they are behaving (teaching, doing research or scholarly writing, raising children, living in neighborhoods, shopping, vacationing, etc.) in very segregated worlds within a narrowly prescribed White normative racial frame (Feagin *White Racial Frame*).

Ironically enough, many White people also do not realize what their protection of their White space is actually costing them in "increased divisiveness," as well as "a distancing from those they perceive as not like them … The ideology of whiteness strips us of our individuality and makes us formulaic representations of what we imagine one another to be" (Babb 168). Humanities professor Valerie Babb, who teaches Whiteness in her classes, continues, "Ultimately, the insularity that whiteness needs to maintain itself—the self-absorbed conversations, the moving only within a set of like people, the exclusive living enclaves—will become difficult to maintain" (171–172). These are the costs that I felt personally, that motivated me to write this book and to reach out to readers and teachers who are no less committed than I am to teaching ethically, fairly, with concern for the success of all students. But I argue that unless we make some personal and institutional changes, we will continue to hamstring ourselves and shortchange our students, all of them.

In composition teaching, despite years of resolutions, guidelines, task forces, dedicated blogs, and special awards, the field is still suffering the evidence of disparate effect in the profession due to race and racism. Notice, for example, that teachers still struggle as a profession to recognize, understand, and appropriately respond to, *African American Vernacular English*, formerly called Black English and incorrect grammar; and *English Language Learners*, formerly called English as a Second Language or English for foreigners, the changing names themselves a pedigree of both the resistance and the hope that people can learn new things.

This struggle with terminology is directly due to the fact that the profession continues to be very White and more often male. The National Center for Education Statistics reports that about 80% of public school teachers were White in 2015–2016. In postsecondary, 41% of faculty were White males and 35% White females. Among full-time professors, 54% were White males and 27% White females, with Black males, Black females, and Hispanic males each comprising 2% in fall 2017 (National Center for Education Statistics "Postsecondary"; National Center for Education Statistics "Public").

Notice, also, a 2010 (the most recent) National Council of Teachers of English Resolution on Social Justice in Education observes that "lack the knowledge, skills, and dispositions to work within schools that have a predominantly urban population". Yet, although the resolution itself addresses the need to support teachers as they teach about differences, and attempts to "acknowledge the vital role" that teacher education plays in preparing teachers to teach about social justice, "advocate" for equitable education policy, and "oppose inequitable learning opportunities," it fails to call for changes in policies and practices that keep the number of teachers of color at very low, sometimes negligible numbers.

As a result, high school and college English and composition classrooms, like the rest of school, are often the site of defacto racism (Feagin *White Racial Frame* 91–122; Pimentel; Sue and Constantine), whether or not teachers are aware or know what to do about it. Instead schools, colleges, and universities, despite presumably best efforts, reproduce and reify the racial achievement gap (Orfield 426–428). Fewer students of color than White make it to high school graduation (Musu-Gillette et al. v), with direct causative links to the mass incarceration of young Black males (Coates 64). Although the racial gap is slowly closing, college graduation, a key to middle class life, is even more elusive for students of color, except Asian students (Musu-Gillette et al. v). In other words, what teachers don't know or do about race has direct negative consequences. As good as teachers are, as inclusive and professional as they try to be, they are still products of the times and places, fragile in their confidence, unsupported in and unprepared to open the Pandora's box of racial topics that pervade their lives. So teachers are more likely to avoid the subject of race than to directly address it in the classrooms at too great a cost to students and society.

As Trainor and others have previously established, our educational institutions, including secondary and postsecondary departments of English, literature, and rhetoric, have codified the racism reflected in other social sites, leaving some serious gaps in curricula and pedagogies. This book grew out of concern for those gaps and their ongoing effect on students, as well as on their teachers. Teachers want and need to understand a student's stage of racial identity and how to respond thoughtfully, with an eye towards developmentally appropriate dialogue, rather than with panic, shock, confusion, or censorious anger. With help, educators can better discern students and their needs, accept their own role as teachers as they also learn, and activate personal and institutional growth towards new understanding of themselves and this confusing world. That is what this book and the following interviews are about.

What I Wish I Had Said

A question I wish I had been brave enough to ask about everything, particularly in my teacher preparation and as I prepped for hundreds of classes, is "Does anyone know the history of that term/situation?" Asking this question provides a way to consider the historical and social knowledge that shapes people's current understanding of racism and privilege. As suggested earlier, White people's lack of experience with and understanding of the lives of people of color, particularly Black people, leads to shocking knowledge gaps and public policy errors that hurt us all. Numerous surveys conducted regularly since the civil rights era of the 1960s show that Whites and Blacks hold opposite views on the extent and consequences to Blacks of job discrimination, housing inequality, and major income gaps, with Whites consistently blaming Black lack of motivation instead of racism and White privilege for racially disparate outcomes (Feagin *Racist America* 123–124). Moreover, the majority of Whites continue to think Blacks have equal access to health care, equal educational access and achievement, comparable employment, and "70 percent of whites were found to hold one or more erroneous beliefs about important white-black differentials in life conditions" (Feagin *White Racial Frame* 2–3).

Blacks and Whites also often don't know their own history or that of other groups. My students were very vocal about their beliefs that racism is a relic of the past, although other than Jefferson's affair with Sally Hemmings, they knew very little about the racism built into the Declaration of Independence and the Constitution; the Native American Trail of Tears and the nature and role of reservations in subjugating native people; the pervasiveness of lynching in the twentieth century; the Jim Crow era; the interment of the Japanese Americans; the role of the FBI in harassing (or worse) Black leaders; federal housing, agriculture, and banking policies that overtly discriminated against Blacks, and much more. Students also didn't know much about Black inventors, scientists, astronauts, industrialists, business leaders, artists, musicians, writers, or White anti-racist allies, all of whom have been crucial to American progress.

In other words, students' were operating in a fact-free historical zone. They had little to no accurate prior knowledge to attach any of their new information to, a crucial feature of how learning works. Without a correction or connection to what they already know, students "inaccurate prior knowledge (in other words, flawed ideas, beliefs, models, or theories) can distort new knowledge by predisposing students to ignore, discount, or resist evidence that conflicts with what they believe to be true" (Ambrose et al. 23–24). As will be discussed in later chapters, my students found the facts so jarring, at times, that they did deny and resist them, and sometimes said they felt severely compromised by what they saw as the lack of honesty on the part of the education system and the adults in their lives who had not told them about White privilege and racism. Repeatedly they'd say, "Why didn't someone tell me?"

The question, "Does anyone know the historical facts of this term/situation?" can be used to help them redress this phenomenon and invite teachers and students to repair the inaccuracies they are suffering in a relatively non-threatening way. And, while the realities are sometimes quite hard to bear, at other times, new understanding can flow most innocently. Once when later students were heatedly engaged in a dialogue about some fact they had not known, a shocked White student kept offensively protesting her innocence, saying, "I never lived around *colored people*! I didn't know that *colored people* were not living the same kind of life I do. I didn't know *colored people* didn't have the same chances." She went on, saying "*colored people* .... *colored people* ..." repeatedly. The room was silent after her outburst and I was weighing the pros and cons of calling her out on her use of "colored people" when an African American student next to her took a big breath and calmly turned to her. "You know," she said, "'colored people' is what people in slave days and Jim Crow times used to call Black people when they weren't calling them the 'n' word, but it still didn't feel good. When you say colored people, I feel like you're putting me back in those days, so could you please not say that?"

"Oh," said the White student. "I didn't know that. No one ever told me. What should I say instead?"

The African American student's response was thoughtful and matter of fact about using "Black" or "African American," and the class opened up to a really informative discussion about identity and how we name people.

No teacher could ask for more, students teaching students, new knowledge synthesized right before our eyes and memorably delivered. I wish I had said that, but then maybe in this case it worked out better to hear it from a student. This book is about teachers developing the courage and the knowledge to accept responsibility for racism when it happens in our classrooms and not have to burden a student, particularly a student of color, with saying what I should have said.

What I have shared in this chapter is only a small part of the proof "out there" that neither the nation nor the field of English have served people of any color very well. People and institutions have made terrible mistakes, both shockingly deliberate and tragically unintentional, and will continue to do so unless educators learn to recognize and undo the racist mechanisms at work. The following interviews provide tangible evidence and practice in recognizing how racism works for typical students, as well as their teachers, myself included. These interviews are offered in humility, hope, and confidence in the intelligence, compassion, and courage of teachers everywhere. Come meet Annabell, Roberta, Elaine, and Madeline and hear what they have to teach us all.

Works Cited

Adams, Maurianne, Lee Anne Bell, and Pat Griffin, eds. *Teaching for Diversity and Social Justice*, 2nd edition. Routledge, 2007.

Adelman, Larry. *Race: The Power of an Illusion*. Film, California Newsreel Independent Television Service, 2003.

Ambrose, Susan A. et al. *How Learning Works: Seven Research-Based Principles for Smart Teaching*. Jossey-Bass, 2010.

Babb, Valerie. *Whiteness Visible: The Meaning of Whiteness in American Literature and Culture*. New York University Press, 1998.

Banning, Marlia E. "The Politics of Resentment." *JAC*, vol. 26, no. 1–2, 2006, pp. 65–101.

Baxter Magolda, Marcia B. and Patricia M. King. *Learning Partnerships: Theory and Models of Practice to Educate for Self-Authorship*. Stylus, 2004.

Bonilla-Silva, Eduardo. "'New Racism,' Color-Blind Racism, and the Future of Whiteness in America." *White Out: The Continuing Significance of Racism*, edited by Ashley Doane and Eduardo Bonilla-Silva. Routledge, 2003, pp. 271–284.

Chesler, Mark A. et al. "Blinded by Whiteness: The Development of White College Students' Racial Awareness." *White Out: The Continuing Significance of Racism*, edited by Ashley Doane and Eduardo Bonilla-Silva. Routledge, 2003, pp. 215–230.

Cieply, Michael. "Academy Board Endorses Changes to Increase Diversity in Oscar Nominees and Itself." *The New York Times*, no. 22 Jan, 2016, http://www.nytimes.com/2016/01/23/business/media/oscars-diversity-academy-voting-rules.html.

Coates, Ta-Nehisi. "The Black Family in the Age of Mass Incarceration." *The Atlantic*, 2015, pp. 60–84.

Daniels, Lee. *Precious*. Film, 2009.

Dargis, Manohla et al. "Oscars So White? Or Oscars So Dumb? Discuss." *The New York Times*, 2016, http://www.nytimes.com/2016/01/24/movies/oscars-so-white-or-oscars-so-dumb-discuss.html?_r=0.

DiAngelo, Robin. *White Fragility*. Beacon Press, 2018.

Feagin, Joe R. *Racist America: Roots, Current Realities, and Future Reparations*. Routledge, 2000.

—. *The White Racial Frame: Centuries of Racial Framing and Counter-Framing*. Routledge, 2010.

Fine, Michelle. "Witnessing Whiteness/Gathering Intelligence." *Off White: Readings on Power, Privilege, and Resistance*, edited by Michelle Fine et al., 2nd edition. Routledge, 2004, pp. 245–256.

George, Ann. "Critical Pedagogy: Dreaming of Democracy." *A Guide to Composition Pedagogies*, edited by Gary Tate et al. Oxford, 2001, pp. 92–112.

Goodburn, Amy. "Racing (Erasing) White Privilege in Teacher/Research Writing About Race." *Race, Rhetoric and Composition*, edited by Keith Gilyard. Boynton/Cook Publishers, 1999, pp. 67–86. *Cross Currents*, Charles I. Schuster.

Gurin, Patricia. "The Expert Report of Patricia Gurin." University of Michigan, 2003. http://www.vpcomm.umich.edu/admissions/legal/expert/gurintoc.html, 11 October 2003.

Haggis, Paul. *Crash*. DVD, 2006.

Hardiman, Rita and Bailey Jackson. "Conceptual Foundations for Social Justice Courses." *Teaching for Diversity and Social Justice: A Sourcebook*, edited by Maurianne Adams et al. Routledge, 1997, pp. 23–29.

Harro, Bobbie. "The Cycle of Socialization." *Readings for Diversity and Social Justice*, edited by Maurianne Adams et al. Routledge, 2000, pp. 15–21.

Helms, Janet E. *Black and White Racial Identity: Theory, Research, and Practice*. Praeger, 1993.

—. "Introduction: Review of Racial Identity Terminology." *Black and White Racial Identity: Theory, Research, and Practice*, edited by Janet E. Helms. Praeger, 1993, pp. 3–8.

—. "Toward a Model of White Racial Identity Development." *Black and White Racial Identity: Theory, Research, and Practice*, edited by Janet E. Helms. Praeger 1993, pp. 49–66.

Houts Picca, Leslie and Joe R. Feagin. *Two-Faced Racism: Whites in the Backstage and the Frontstage*. Routledge, 2007.

Johnson, Leanor Boulin and Robert Staples. *Black Families at the Crossroads: Challenges and Prospects*. revised edition. Jossey-Bass, 2005.

King, Joyce E. "Dysconcious Racism: Ideology, Identity, and the Miseducation of Teachers." *Journal of Negro Education*, vol. 60, no. 2, 1991, pp. 133–146.

LaGravanese, Richard. *Freedom Writers*. IMDb, 2007.

McIntosh, Peggy. "White Privilege and Male Privilege: A Personal Account of Coming to See Correspondences through Work in Women's Studies " *Working Paper*, Center for Research on Women, Wellesley College, 1988.

McIntyre, Alice. *Making Meaning of Whiteness: Exploring Racial Identity with White Teachers*. State University of New York Press, 1997.

Musu-Gillette, Lauren et al. "Status and Trends in the Education of Racial and Ethnic Groups 2016." National Center for Education Statistics, Institute of Education Science, U.S. Department of Education, 2016. http://nces.ed.gov/pubsearch;http://nces.ed.gov/pubsearch, 25 Aug 2016.

National Center for Education Statistics. *Characteristics of Postsecondary Faculty*. U.S. Department of Education, Institute for Education Sciences May 2019 Accessed 1 July 2019.

—. "Characteristics of Public School Teachers." U.S. Department of Education, Institute of Education Sciences April 2018 Accessed 1 July 2019.

National Council of Teachers of English. "Resolution on Social Justice in Literacy Education." *NCTE Position Statement*. National Council of Teachers of English http://ncte.org/positions/statements/socialjustice. Accessed 24 August 2016.

Orfield, Myron. "Milliken, Meredith, and Metropolitan Segregation." *UCLA Law Review*, vol. 62, no. 364, 2015.

Pew Research Center. "By 2055, the U.S. Will Have No Racial or Ethnic Majority Group." 23 Sept 2015 http://www.pewhispanic.org. Accessed 9 Aug 2016.

Pimentel, Octavio. "Invitation to a Too-Long Postponed Conversation: Race and Composition." *Reflections: Public Rhetoric, Civic Writing, and Service Learning*, vol. 12, no. 2, 2013, pp. 90–109.

Pruitt, Linda Powell. "The Achievement (K)Not: Whiteness and 'Black Underachievement'." *Off White: Readings on Power, Privilege, and Resistance*, edited by Michelle Fine et al., 2nd edition, Routledge, 2004, pp. 235–244.

Ratcliffe, Krista. *Rhetorical Listening: Identification, Gender, Whiteness*. Southern Illinois University Press, 2005. *Studies in Rhetorics and Feminisms*, Shirley Glenn and Shirley Wilson Logan.

Rosenberg, Pearl M. "Color Blindness in Teacher Education: An Optical Delusion." *Off White: Readings on Power, Privilege, and Resistance*, edited by Michelle Fine et al., 2nd edition. Routledge, 2004, pp. 257–272.

Sommers, Nancy and Laura Saltz. "The Novice as Expert: Writing the Freshman Year." *College Composition and Communication*, vol. 56, no. 1, 2004, pp. 124–149.

Sue, Derald Wing. *Race Talk and the Conspiracy of Silence*. John Wiley & Sons, Inc., 2015.

Sue, Derald Wing and Madonna G. Constantine. "Racial Microaggressions as Instigators of Difficult Dialogues on Race: Implications for Student Affairs Educators and Students." *The College Student Affairs Journal*, vol. 26, no. 2, 2007, pp. 136–143, EBSCOhost Integrated Search.

Sugrue, Thomas. "Expert Report of Thomas J. Sugrue: Separate Worlds: Residential Segregation and Racial Isolation." University of Michigan 4 Sept 2003 https://repository.law.umich.edu/mjrl/vol5/iss1/13/Accessed 23 Oct 2014.

Swim, Janet K. and Deborah L. Miller. "White Guilt: Its Antecedents and Consequences for Attitudes toward Affirmative Action." *Personality and Social Psychology Bulletin*, vol. 25, no. 4, April 1999, pp. 500–514, Sage Full-Text Collections. Union Institute & University.

Tatum, Beverly Daniel. *"Why Are All the Black Kids Sitting Together in the Cafeteria?" And Other Conversations About Race*. Basic Books, 2003.

The Education Week Research Center. "U.S. Graduation Rate Reaches a New High." *Education Week*, vol. 35, no. 33, 2016, p. 32, EbscoHost.

Trainor, Jennifer Seibel. "Critical Pedagogy's Other: Constructions of Whiteness in Education for Social Change." *College Composition and Communication*, vol. 53, no. 4, 2002, pp. 631–650.

—. "From Identity to Emotion: Frameworks for Understanding, and Teaching against, Anticritical Sentiments in the Classroom." *JAC*, vol. 26, no. 3–4, 2006, pp. 643–655.

—. *Rethinking Racism: Emotion, Persuasion, and Literacy Education in an All-White High School*. Southern Illinois University Press, 2008.

Yakin, Boaz. *Remember the Titans*. Film, IMDb, 2000.

Zinn, Howard. *A People's History of the United States 1492–Present*. HarperCollins Publishers, 2001.

· 3 ·

ANNABELL

There are few joys in life that rival a teacher's experience of smart, eager students. The sheer fun of teaching such students can be almost orgasmic; they make our jobs easier and often draw the best from us as educators and mentors. But they can also reward us in insularity, a certain pedagogical myopia, believing we are doing a good job because they continue to bounce in their seats with enthusiasm. Perhaps speaking for myself, although I suspect otherwise, it is tempting to just keep the "good" student happy, to prod her gently to take only a few steps out of her comfort zone, allowing her to slide back to where she feels in greater control (and has always gotten good grades before). In this chapter, I'd like to explore the experience of just such a student and, through her comments from interviews when she was a first-year student and then again as a senior, examine the dynamics of a "good" student who is asked to go further outside of her comfort zone. At the same time, I will raise questions about my role as teacher and about the role of my institution in helping me and such students embark on that journey that has implications for their lives and the part the institution may (or not) play in building a just society.

Annabell is one of the five students whose voices ground the theory of this book. I use sociologists Baxter Magolda and King's theory of self-authorship as the context for a discussion of Annabell's racial identity development, gleaned from her interview to illustrate how students (and teachers) like Annabell make sense of their encounters with new information about racism, Whiteness, and privilege. I also examine Annabell's responses using other theories of racial identity development, resistance, the role of emotion, race traitors, and bystander intervention.

Annabell is an example of the student who relishes the intellectual challenge of studying racism through writing. Perhaps unconsciously, she sidesteps the emotional challenges to her White identity and yet is attracted to an anti-racist identity, with seeming disregard for the rending of emotional attachments to previous understanding and friendships that rested on privilege. Instead, she dives into the intellectual challenge of crafting a new identity that better acknowledges the racism and its privilege, and firmly rejects her association with it.

But Annabell also typifies the incomplete accommodation to this new identity. At times, she resists the information, indulging in denial and disbelief, demanding a high level of proof before accepting the facts. She also distances herself from privilege by showing how she is different from other (White) students. Ironically, her differentiating herself becomes her activism by the time she is a college senior in ways I find very reminiscent of myself as instructor. Thus together, she and I illustrate an intellectualized approach to activism that both students and teachers practice to shape a new anti-racist White identity.

Cognitive Maturity and Differentiation

Annabell, a White twenty-something with dark hair and trendy black-rimmed eyeglasses, often has a thoughtful, almost mischievous look in her eyes when considering ideas or questions. She graduated as a criminal justice major and was one of the few students in the first-year class who was not from within 50 miles of the university. I recall her remarking on the impact of this once, saying that being from out of town accounted for the difference in her perspective on some things. In one discussion she turned to one of her classmates who'd just confessed to not believing that racism was still a problem in our society and said, "You need to get out more!"

Annabell felt her early life with a diverse group of friends had prepared her to be more accepting of some of the anti-racist readings and discussion of the course. In the first-year and senior interviews, she said she felt she was lucky to have had such a close, diverse group of friends for such a long time, even from elementary, "where more of my friends were either African American or Hispanic or Puerto Rican. We didn't really discuss it but they had necklaces that said Puerto Rico but they never talked about it." She was disappointed that at the university, "My friend group is not as diverse as I would like it to be. I can count on one hand the number who have any kind of ethnic diversity at all." A positive early experience with difference created an expectation in her that she would grow more in that way at college, which perhaps predisposed her to be receptive to the course content.

Further demonstrating her mental and social agility, she also expressed her good fortune at being a criminal justice major in my writing class; the connections were easy and motivating to her. She felt she was getting a "two-fer" and pitied her classmates who couldn't see the connection to their majors in biology or business. This interdisciplinary capacity is a marker of her cognitive maturity and integrated identity (Baxter Magolda and King 7), discussed later.

Moving Through and Past Resistance

Although Annabell clearly differentiated herself from her classmates whose ideas and experiences she felt were far narrower than hers, she did find her own ways to resist the content of the course. Annabell often challenged what we had to say in class, whether it was something I said or another student's words. She wanted the proof, the numbers behind an assertion. She herself would often research an idea outside of class time, wanting more documentation of racial discrimination in housing or health care, for example, as if she couldn't believe it was as bad as the course material said. Even as she sifted the evidence, she was sometimes shocked at what she found in her research and then tried to make sense of the new information. She often said, "I didn't know! … I can't believe it! … Why is this still …? Wait, this doesn't make sense." This kind of denial is the first and perhaps the most commonly experienced on the list of resistances Ratcliffe identifies among her own students when they encounter critical pedagogy (138).

But even as she struggled in the gap between what she was learning and her previous knowledge, Annabell was not threatened by the new information as were some of her peers like Elaine or even Roberta, instead finding voice for her ideas in the writing we did in the course. She said she felt newly empowered in "learning to write about things that you have no idea about, or you never wanted to write about before, and … stretching your comfort zone, and being more like a professional writer rather than, like a selfish writer … more flexible." She was aware that being able to build an essay from the ideas at hand, even if they were new or not immediately interesting to her, were marks of new generative skill and accomplishment for them as writers and critical thinkers. Imagine a student on fire with learning, hungry for more, particularly anything that related to her specialty, criminal justice. Thus, her final research paper in the first-year composition class was on racial bias in the death penalty.

Annabell described the necessity of having to write about race repeatedly as an important motivator to deeper thinking about the topic:

> Um, I would say that it maybe made me work a little harder just because … I had to find a way to make it more narrow, more focused, rather than … let's write about race. Like, "okay, well, now let me break it down. How can I write about it this way?" So you had to be more focused to keep it about race and another topic at the same time …

While having experienced the first-year assignment as a problem, Annabell also described in the first-year interview how the pedagogy encouraged her to learn to make connections across categories of knowledge she had formerly seen as distinct. This is a kind of synergistic thinking that she realized she might have been able to avoid without the requirement that she write about race more than once, as she might in another kind of composition course. Perhaps it is this "sustained involvement" with a single topic that has accelerated her growth from "novice" to "expert," to use Harvard writing professors Sommers' and Saltz's terms (147), although that outcome would require further study to corroborate. In spite of the radical differences she found between what she thought she knew before about race and her new learning, she seemed fearless, riding the rapids, thrilled there was something new to be learned. And, unlike many of her peers, she didn't seem bothered that the new learning directly challenged long-held beliefs, as long as she could see the intellectual proof.

Through another theoretical lens, Annabell is beginning to "view knowledge as contextual" (Baxter Magolda and King 12) as illustrated in her comments above, which lays the foundation for her to see the information on racism and privilege as a partial frame of reference for her experiences and insights. During her college career, beginning with the race-themed composition course, she came to understand that her previous knowledge about race was incomplete, lacking other frames of reference outside of her experience. This new awareness caused her to relinquish her "reliance on authority as a source of knowledge" and turn to an "Evolving awareness and acceptance of uncertainty and multiple perspectives" and to "recognize need to take responsibility for choosing beliefs" (Baxter Magolda and King 12).

Instead of feeling that the new information threatened her personal identity, she saw herself as empowered to take in the new information and incorporate it in her own revised system of internal belief. Her personal identity could respond to the new information by floating in it or above it; the new information did not threaten the integrity of her intrapersonal foundation, again according to Baxter Magolda and King (8). Rather, her intrapersonal foundation could encompass the new information without losing integrity.

In the same way, the new information that racism still exists and that she personally possessed White privilege did not destroy her interpersonal foundation either. Instead of turning away from the information and the people who were different from herself, she turned towards the new experience, "mutually negotiating needs, and genuinely taking others' perspectives into account without being consumed by them" (Baxter Magolda and King 10). When faced with information that challenged her racial identity and interracial relationships, she did more research on her topic, sought diverse relationships off-campus where there was greater racial diversity, and eventually became romantically involved with a biracial boyfriend. In other words, she sought greater immersion in information and relationship, which further built her epistemological and intrapersonal foundations, and contributed to increased cognitive maturity, integrated identity, mature relationship, and its outcomes: effective citizenship and, ultimately self-authorship (Baxter Magolda and King 7–8).

Struggling with Resistance, Relying on Logic

It is interesting to note, at the same time, that even as Annabell recognized the change in her thinking, she was also subtly engaged in denial of the overarching nature of race, racism, and privilege, its presence and influence in every "topic." Instead she maintained the privileged construction that race is only a topic when the writer chooses. This belief is a form of resistance to a basic premise of the course as well as a logical flaw in her thinking.

Annabell also saw herself branching from one area of interest to another under the broad topic of race, a strategy that she attributed to her major (criminal justice) having many racial tangents that she could explore, unlike, she believed, other students' majors:

> And then, I know that a lot of people were getting really frustrated, that everything was on race. Um, at first I was kind of like, how am I going to come up with seven different topics that are all about racism? But, since my major is criminal justice and sociology, it was easier for me because there are things that I'm interested in to write about. But if someone else doesn't really have any perspective on the world, if all they're interested in is like, math, they're not going to have a million different ways to change it, so they're going to feel like they're writing about the same thing every time. Whereas at least I felt like I was writing about something different every time. And I was writing about something related to criminal justice, and tying in race, rather than writing about race and tying in criminal justice or something.

Although Annabell didn't see that any major could potentially have multiple relationships or topics related to race (perhaps another expression of her denial/resistance), she at least saw the process in her own familiar territory. Unaware of her own relative cognitive maturity and epistemological foundation, which allowed her to move more easily between different frames of reference (Baxter Magolda and King 8), she assumed that other students' difficulties were their bad luck in choice of majors rather than their lesser skills in autonomy and self-authorship, to use the parlance of student development.

Annabell loved gathering information, seeing herself as a sleuth in pursuit of facts and data. Three of the four students made comments in the interviews related to their understanding of how evidence contributed rhetorically to their essays. They all noted the persuasive power of expert resources, realizing, as Annabell did, "it's kind of hard to ignore [when there are] a lot of facts and when everything's pointing in one way." She told of a related discussion in another course, Deviant Behavior, about the criminal penalties for crack and powder cocaine, and how her knowledge of facts and data from the composition course's study of race helped her in the criminal justice course:

> [I]n that class we actually discussed a lot of things like the profiles for who's most likely to commit this crime and why, and theories behind it, and all sorts of things. Kind of like -- African American males are more likely than other groups of people to commit certain crimes more often than others, and it's like, well why? And it helped to kind of have those two classes going at the same time cause it kind of gave you a background of information for both things. And we discussed the crack versus

> cocaine laws specifically. And I was like, "Oh, I know, I know," and I kept volunteering a lot of information, so, I was definitely glad that I knew about it.

Annabell was empowered by the information, raising critical questions in confidence that the research will stand up to further scrutiny because she had seen it work that way in her own writing. She felt it important to test her arguments and her writing, describing a time when she used her hall-mates as a proxy audience:

> We'd all be doing homework together and I'd be like, "what -- what am I writing about again? What is the topic? How am I supposed to do this?" And then asking them questions sort of "Do you really think this is racism? Like do you think I can prove that it is, or does it sound like I'm just going to turn information and make it sound like I'm writing it?" Or I'd ask about a question because … I don't know … to make sure I was on the right track, I guess, understanding the assignment right and interpreting what I was reading, research-wise. Like, if I read this out loud, does this make sense to you?

Annabell thrived in rhetorical approaches that emphasized logos, finding a firm footing in research-based responses to racial dilemmas inherent in contemporary social ills. She rejected "softer" approaches to knowledge, such as the self-reflective journals that often served as prewriting to the research-based essays.

Her report of her resistance to writing the journals is typical of many students' initial denial of Whiteness and its implications: she felt the second journal assignment to write about her race or ethnicity "doesn't mean anything! What am I supposed to write? This is outrageous! There aren't any guidelines. What am I supposed to write?" After consulting with her classmates, she interpreted their advice as "'… you just write something.' And, I'm like, 'All right.'" The resulting narrative about being the only White girl in her grade school class revealed moderate defensiveness against the idea that she might have some of the White privilege that one of their readings described, Peggy McIntosh's famous "invisible weightless knapsack of special provisions, maps, passports, codebooks, visas, clothes, tools, and blank checks" (McIntosh), all afforded her because she is White. Thus, Annabell did write the assignment but displayed "indifferent compliance," another form of resistance (Ratcliffe 138) to the critical race pedagogy of the course and/or to learning from more qualitative experiences.

Annabell's response to the journals can be read in at least two ways: (1) testimony to White students' perceived lack of racial identity, or (2) evidence of her lack of trust in qualitative methods. She sometimes weighed evidence, lined up in a two-column, pro-con list, confident that the world sorted neatly along a binary and that she had arranged it fairly, apples to apples, paving the way for definitive answers and argumentative stances. When the tally indicated a preponderance of this evidence on one side, as she judged it, the direction was clear to her, and she would not relinquish her research and deliberation until she arrived at that clarity.

Often, her arguments were well considered and strongly supported, providing a rationale for the rejection of the death penalty, for example. However, her insistence on the importance of having the preponderance of evidence in one's favor in order to accept a racial critique sometimes virtually Whitewashed important contravening evidence that was more orange to her apple. If the proof was untidy or inconclusive, whether or not it raised possibly significant issues, she set it aside, and proceeded, justified, to her more satisfying conclusion. Her resistance to self-reflection, qualitative information from others' experience, and incomplete but troubling data revealed her own insecurity about (resistance to) the study of racism, in spite of her professed anti-racist stance.

Annabell seemed to find emotional safety in rationalizing an encounter with unexpected information about race and the persistence of racism, even in her own beliefs. She used the language of critical thinking processes to objectify the experience. At one point, she narrated her thinking process as she conducted research on racial bias in the death penalty, recognizing its institutional roots: "So, then it's kind of like, well, why is this going unnoticed, or why isn't it being changed, and then it's like frustration with, maybe the government, rather than yourself or other people, and – I don't know, I can't really …." In answering a follow-up question, Annabell clarified that she realized that she had shifted her criticism from individuals to institutions and systems. An institutional focus is a more sophisticated and complex understanding of how subtle racism operates in today's society, as opposed to the dominant discourse that focuses on the reduction of interpersonal, overt expressions of prejudice, such as through the Ku Klux Klan.

While the recognition of the institutionalization of racism is a goal of the course, it also provides White students with an "out," a safe, logical haven, removing racism to at least an arm's length from themselves. It's someone else's fault, and they are still good people because they can see and critique the racism. This tactic forestalls and moderates the emotional havoc of finding racism in themselves, allowing them to continue the uncloaking of racial injustice, nudging their complacent privilege but not toppling their identities as basically good people. At the juncture of old identity and new information, where guilt could flood, swirl, and topple the raft, students like Annabell use critical thinking as an oar to steady the craft, easing the entry into new waters with a Sherlock Holmesian eye for the intellectually interesting aspects of cognitive dissonance, rather than overturning in emotional whitewater.

Annabell was aware that she was not entirely immune, though, to the emotional components of the class. Like most of the students in the course, she liked the video series, *Race: The Power of an Illusion*, and especially the viewing of the film *Crash* with the student residents of the Intercultural House, a race-themed college residence option nearby. Students may like the two video experiences because the films provide them with models of other, anti-racist ways to be White, an important facet of the immersion/emersion stage on Helms's White identity scale (62). Annabell considered the joint film viewing a bonding experience for the group, noting that it is interesting to hear what everyone thinks after having seen the same movie; she believed that the difficulty in race discussions comes from a lack of common ground, where "everyone's coming from a completely different … experiences in their past, or different understanding of things, and … everyone's at a different point on the issue in their life, or whatever it is. So discussions can be difficult to have." She commented that in some discussions, she felt brought down by others' negativity about the topic, once again revealing her own bias towards neat resolution and positivism. It was not clear if "negativity" referred to the resistance of other students to finding common ground or to her own struggle with and resistance to the complexity of the topics of racism, privilege, and Whiteness.

Moving towards Activism and Self-Authorship

It is interesting to consider the nature of the change in Annabell's resistance. When I interviewed her in her first year, she described mixed feelings about the effect that class had had on her as an anti-racist. She explained she would speak out or intervene if the situation demanded it, but also felt it only prudent to maintain a certain distance (read: resistance). She didn't identify with any resolution for future action that she felt was too radical in a situation that might have called on her to act:

> Um, I don't think I necessarily displayed it [intention] or said it out loud, but I had maybe internal thoughts or something. And I wouldn't say anything really drastic, but more like just to keep an open mind, or try to see multiple sides of things more often, and kind of just be more aware of what's going on around me.

This new concern that there might be something to *be* aware of appears to be a direct result of her encounter with surprising information about racial profiling and unfair discrepancies in crack and powder cocaine laws and enforcement practices. Yet, although she feels she is more aware of the racial aspects of her and others' experiences, she still resists fully engaging, doing something "drastic" in response. Lawrence and Tatum refer to this stance as pseudo-independence, which, although displaying more awareness of the privilege and power associated with Whiteness, is still hampered by its "'power evasive' orientation." They borrow Frankenberg's terminology in describing this attitude as, "a status consistent with 'White liberal' thinking about race and characterized by avoidance of responsibility for racial inequality and injustice" (Lawrence and Tatum 366). Still Annabell's desire by the end of the first-year course to be less resistant and more aware is an intellectual commitment three stages ahead of the color-blindness she seemed to profess at the start.

Despite her first-year avoidance of "drastic" action, as a senior, Annabell was very cognizant of how race works in her social and work lives. In fact, in the senior interview, she said it was important to notice race and to call it to others' attention. For example, she told the story of being the only White person working at Gwen's Girls, a program to support disadvantaged girls socially and academically. The girls nick-named her Snowflake, teasing her about her Whiteness, which she accepted and did not find threatening, as many other White people would. Again, this response evidences Annabell's strongly integrated identity and an interpersonal foundation that allows her "to engage in interdependent relationships with diverse others in which self is not overshadowed by a need for others' approval, mutually negotiating needs, and generally taking others' perspectives into account without being consumed by them" (Baxter Magolda and King 8). She viewed the girls' nickname as friendly, not demeaning, and understood their needs to acknowledge her racial difference but tug at her authority a little for social parity.

In another story about negotiating race in her life, she noted in her "old job" as a food server at the country club, "There were only two African American servers and the rest were in the kitchen," identifying a common employment pattern of Blacks being confined to the lowest status jobs available. She told the story of her earliest days at her new office job:

> So, then at work, at the current job I started two weeks ago, actually at my very first day, I went home and talked to my roommate and I was like, "Well everyone is 30 years old and White. Everyone in the whole office is White." It surprised me. I wasn't surprised that I noticed but every time I told someone they'd say, "Who notices that on their first day of work?" but I was telling them how many women there were, the whole demographic breakdown.

Annabell's heightened awareness of who was in the room and her willingness to say it out loud broke the taboos associated with noticing race, resisting White people's tendency to frame themselves positively as "good and virtuous" (Feagin 96) in spite of their words and actions that demonstrate deficits in their racial competency. Annabell's activism provided counter-cultural resistance to the dominant narrative of color-blindness among Whites (Feagin 97), resisting the normativity of segregated White spaces (Houts Picca and Feagin 262). Her willingness to speak up is also counter to a perceived female norm of begin a passive bystander in which, "While white women often seem uncomfortable with racist comments and other actions, they usually do nothing to counter them, often saying with resignation, 'Oh well, he'll never change'" (Houts Picca and Feagin 80). It should be noted here, though, that other research by these authors found that "white women are more likely to actively disrupt racist performances" (Houts Picca and Feagin 262), so Annabell is among that number. Again, her self-authorship empowers her "to internally define a coherent belief system and identity that coordinates mutual relations with others" (Baxter Magolda and King 8), an uncommon status among her peers.

She also resisted racism in her social life by calling out others on their racist, sexist, and homophobic jokes. In the senior interview, she talked about how she has grown into this stance:

> The thing that's changed the most is that I will start discussions about anything really, not just race. But if someone makes a comment about gender or is homophobic, I will say, Oh, did you notice there was only one woman in there or did you notice that people were watching as we walked in the store? People constantly tell jokes. It drives me insane that if there are only White people in the room, they are going to tell any kind of joke, Jewish jokes a lot. I have so many Jewish friends and I'll say something. It doesn't make sense because a lot of Jewish people are White, so they don't know that I'm not Jewish but they know I'm not Black. My ex-boyfriend--people didn't know that he was half Black and people would say things in front of him. People assume that everyone in the room is White and Catholic or Christian, and they tell jokes all the time at parties. I'm always the person who is the stick in the

> mud. I'm like, "You're offending me so I'm gonna go in the other room." I don't cause a scene but I'm like, "No, I just don't find it funny."

Without realizing it, Annabell has duplicated the observations of Houts Picca, Feagin and others who have written about the "backstage" phenomenon, in which an in-group, generally White people, slip into racism more easily when they believe there are no out-group members present.

For example, Whites will tell racist jokes about Blacks, Jews, Asians, Latinos, gays, people with handicaps, etc. when they believe only people like themselves—able-bodied, heterosexual Whites—are in the room (Houts Picca and Feagin 68–74). In the senior interview, Annabell further reported the following:

> People will say comments that they think they are saying to an all-White room … Something I always hear when someone makes a racist comment and I'll call them out on it and they'll say, "I'm not racist. I have Black friends." Without missing a beat. Everytime I can predict what they are gonna say. Usually if it's a Black joke or they'll tell gay jokes and they'll say, "Well I have a gay friend, I don't hate gay people." And I'm like well would you tell that joke if your gay friend was here? And usually they'll say yes, but then I'll say do you think he is comfortable or he just doesn't want to make a scene? I'm always the joke ruiner. So we have discussions about whether we should say something. I always think that if it's just me personally, that I want to say something just because everyone thinks I'm overreacting. It just makes them think about, for just a minute. And at the end of the day everyone may be making fun of how sensitive I am, but at least they are talking about that someone got upset about it. So I know sometimes I'm overreacting and I know sometimes it doesn't always have to be said. That's what everyone tells me. But I'd rather it be discussed. I'd rather spend 20 minutes talking about how I'm overreacting. At least we're talking about it, I guess.

Her party experience loosely parallels a report from one of Picca and Feagin's journal narratives of a student who was part of their large inter-university study. The student, Carter, describes a dorm party he attended with friends:

> Normally there is not a large proportion of minorities at parties we have attended, but there were many African Americans at this one. One of my friends, Rob, commented that "This is a rather dark party." I noticed this and was very offended, and this only grew when he then commented, "Quick, hide all the white girls." I mustered some courage and told him he shouldn't make stereotypical and racist comments. He then said, "Sorry, I didn't mean to offend anyone." I think that just goes to show that many people don't realize what they say can be deemed offensive, and oftentimes do not think before they speak. (262)

Like Carter, Annabell's interruption of negative comments and racist, sexist and homophobic jokes set her apart from her peers who think jokes and comments are harmless. Although she said she "doesn't cause a scene," and clings to the dominant narrative that she is "overreacting" by noting racism, she was drawing attention to an alternative perspective and thereby interrupting racism/sexism/homophobia, thus creating a safer space for others to speak out also. This kind of action has the potential to change the dominant norm, as psychologists, sociologists and health educators have found in other kinds of bystander intervention (Fabiano et al.).

Teachers as Cautious Activists

I must admit I used to identify with Annabell's approach to change and greater consciousness that I call "the cautious activist." Annabell, myself, and students and teachers like her prefer a measured, intellectual stance, filtering information that might threaten the racial identity through a logic filter held at arm's length, a safe distance from the heart. Balance and the ability to keep the craft upright through stormy waters are higher values than full openness to new information and experience. Cautious activists find affirmation in critiquing institutional and personal racism but moderating the emotional intake and proceeding slowly and carefully towards change in the status quo. As a result, they avoid anything "drastic," such as relinquishing privilege, but remain observant, often from the sidelines.

Obviously, this less-than-wholehearted embrace of an anti-racist identity indicates an unfinished project, which continues to cry for progress and reform. For myself, I am struck nearly mute by the question, "How integrated is my life?" Like my students, I don't want to be that bad person who resists social justice for others. But there are times when I am stymied how to create a sufficient change, to recognize even what that change might entail and at what point it could be sufficient. The awareness that people must change themselves and create change around them is the blessing and the peril of teaching and learning anti-racism. Once teachers are aware of their privileged complicity in the pain others suffer, they can't return to ignorance. For the instructor who has become aware of her personal privilege, the desire to dismantle it becomes an ethical obligation in her teaching that has its own dilemmas.

The Effects of Instructor Authorities

Although the student and instructor both experience the anti-racist class as an intellectual and emotional journey, it is a different journey for each, not just because of experiences, styles, values, and strategies each bring, but because of the power differential. Annabell was one of three interviewed students who addressed, either directly or indirectly, my power as an instructor, and sometimes ascribing that I have additional credibility as a *White* instructor talking about race, racism, and privilege, power that they would not award an instructor of color. Other educators, including some of my African American colleagues, have noted how some White students directly question the authority of the instructor of color, particularly when s/he talks about race (Elias and Jones 8; Espinosa-Aguilar 152–53; TuSmith).

In response to the interview question, "What impact, if any, do you feel the instructor's race had on the class and your response to this class?" Annabell uncritically narrated this bias toward the White instructor:

> Well, I guess if the instructor would have been African American … People probably would have been just like, "That's just her personal opinion," or, "They're just biased," or whatever. But since it was a person from a completely different race talking about racism in a different race, it was more like, "Oh, well, maybe she's right, maybe." [I]t would make you think about it more; whereas if the person was discussing their own race –or even if you were up there being like, "Well, White people are discriminated against. Here's how. It happened to me this time …" you're just like wow – she's just had bad luck and now she's angry about it …. So it really was like, oh, okay, well if she noticed then maybe there's something there ….

Annabell privileged the White instructor with an objectivity that she (or said others would have) denied the African American instructor. Again distancing herself from her classmates, she differentiated herself from others' less-informed views, but her subsequent description of the White instructor's power to distort information for a desired effect (White guilt) reveals her deeper belief that instructors do manipulate information for their own purposes, even if the goal may be a worthy one:

> But … so I could see how that [instructor's race] would maybe affect it, but personally, it didn't really change much for me. Some people might see it from this perspective, of … you're going out of your way to find it … because a White person might be going out of their way to find it because they feel bad about it, or the society has told them that there's racism everywhere, so it's like, well, "I think there is, and I'm going to find it" … being self-righteous almost because you feel you want to do something so good

> because you owe it to those people ... I didn't really have any of those reactions, but I would think that would maybe be the only influences on the class, the way people might look at it ... because the class was more on writing, so to constantly talk about race is, ... wow, why are we constantly talking about it? But if it was ... a racial class ... if you went into it knowing, oh, we're going to discuss differences in cultures or this and this ... it wouldn't really affect anything, maybe. I don't know. I think I just babbled a lot, now.

Having directly challenged the instructor's authority to make transparent the racial content in a writing course, Annabell back-pedaled at the end of her comment, again deferring to my authority, softening the blow, as if to say, "But who am I to criticize?" So, the awareness of the instructor's power is there, even as she addressed me. She poked at it a little, but was careful not to provoke the teacher-monster, again displaying her cautious activist approach.

On the other hand, if Annabell's comments are read from a student perspective, she may simply not feel safe enough to say what she truly feels, a phenomenon others have noted in their studies of critical classrooms (Espinosa-Aguilar 155). Still another reading of this portion of the interview may be more positive and indicate a certain amount of maturity as a writer, rather than deferring to my authority. Annabell may, instead, be taking the "nonjudgmental stance" of "connected knowing" as famed human development specialist Mary Field Belenky and her colleagues in women's studies describe the responses of some of their students, contrasting the male and female response styles:

> Women seem to take naturally to a nonjudgmental stance. In teaching undergraduates we have found it necessary to ask many of the males to refrain from making judgments until they understood the topic. On the other hand, we have often had to prod the females into critical examination. Even when they disagreed vehemently with an opinion, they hesitated to judge it wrong until they had tried to understand the reasoning behind it. (116)

Perhaps Annabell's deference to me was not to my authority as a teacher but as another person as she performed the role of connected knower who was considering how to negotiate "some sort of integration of feeling and thinking" (Belenky et al. 130). So this passage could be read as an enactment of a female dynamic rather than a power dynamic, although the two often intersect in U.S. culture.

Although as a first-year student, Annabell said she would not do anything "drastic" when confronted with racism, her actions as a senior are indeed radical in their attack on the foundations of racism, which is fostered, nurtured, and sustained by in-group comments and jokes that further institutionalize difference from White as a deficit (Fine 246) and make Whiteness and its privilege more invisible as a racial construct (Ratcliffe 112–113).

While Annabell realized she had changed, she downplayed that shift, perhaps out of modesty or a reticence to reject completely those (often friends) who continue to perpetrate the racism, sexism, or homophobia. Her expressed desire to have a more diverse group of friends could provide her, and others like her, the support to continue to be a "race traitor," to use sociologist Mark Patrick George's term. Perhaps hearkening to her memories of the diversity she experienced as a younger child, Annabell's activism seemed to express an intent to actively recreate a "cosmopolitan canopy" in which "Diverse people converge, defining the setting as belonging to everyone and deemphasizing race and other particularities. No one group claims priority" (Anderson 5). Sociologist Elijah Anderson's ethnographic study of places in Philadelphia models an anti-racist future for us all, where the cosmopolitan canopy can

> … provide an opportunity for diverse strangers to become acquainted with people they otherwise seldom observe up close. The existence of the canopy allows such people, whose stronger reference point often remains their own social class or ethnic group, a chance to encounter others and so work toward a more cosmopolitan appreciation of difference. (276)

Annabell appears to be seeking such a cosmopolitan canopy, a like-minded peer group, an emotionally and intellectually congruent community that will scaffold the anti-racist change she wants to be part of in society.

There is yet another aspect of Annabell's responses to racism that stands out. Trainor explains that the "role of emotion in learning and in ideological processes have made clear that emotions are central to how we process our political beliefs and formulate rational understandings of the social world …" (22). Yet Annabell's preferred style and method of resistance is intellectualization, "avoiding unacceptable emotions by focusing on the intellectual aspects" (Watt et al. 97) of an issue or dilemma. Students (and faculty) like her find refuge in distancing from the emotions necessary to the personal integration of a new anti-racist identity. It is a functional, pragmatic approach for the classroom, allowing students and faculty to moderate their cognitive and emotional dissonance. But Trainor is saying that such emotional disconnects will slow and even negate the students' (teachers') ability to recognize and integrate their racial identities, responsibilities, and opportunities.

It is important that universities provide safe havens and supportive space for people like Annabell to recognize and own responsibility for privilege and disparate racial outcomes, including both cognitive and emotional work; to deconstruct normative judgments of difference; to interrupt racist incidents and conversations on campus and in their communities of comfort, and thus dismantle subtle and not-so-subtle institutional racism. How can students be enthusiastically and meaningfully invited and encouraged to explore their own racial identities, developing the competencies, personal clarity, and relationships that will help them to self-authorship in their lives, their work, and their futures? How can faculty, particularly White faculty, be supported in their own cognitive and emotional work, across the curriculum, in ways that invite commitment to conversation and growth rather than guilt-ridden, required diversity training that is perceived as a punitive external demand? How can colleges and universities become "cosmopolitan canopies," beacons of hope and knowledge about effective and rewarding ways to "do" race in our neighborhoods, communities, and nation? Annabell's work and the work of students and faculty like her, although incomplete, model, inspire, and challenge us to learn the skills we need to teach self-authorship in the context of racial identity, and to scrutinize our educational institutions for practices and policies that undermine Annabell's courage and passion to learn more and live more fully. I believe we owe her that.

What I Wish I Had Said

While it doesn't work easily for every student, intellectually-oriented students like Annabell are especially receptive to returning to a text—a reading, a film—and mining its precise evidence to support or refute an argument. For them, the question, "Where does the reading (or film) say that?" encourages a welcome return to text that the teacher has specifically chosen; they know there is information in there and they are motivated to find it. Reminding students to return to the text for "answers" gives them guidance and authority for their thinking, even when their (new) thoughts run counter to previously held beliefs. Bolgatz, an experienced high school teacher and college education professor, also directs attention to the power of "explicitly modeling and giving students the language to question each other." She recalls a teacher who consistently reminded students to ask, "What do you mean?" and "How do you know?" (70). Though broader, these questions have the same purpose of challenging students to examine evidence critically beyond their own knee-jerk, emotionally or socially derived opinion.

Annabell also found power, affirmation, and an unexpected sense of community in the group experience of the film, *Crash*. Like the language modeling that Bolgatz refers to, Annabell delighted in the opportunity to engage in passionate discussion with older students (she was in her first year, they were at sophomore through grad level) who clearly liked to think and were unafraid to challenge the ideas, assumptions, prejudices, and emotions generated by the film. The film's willingness to examine the dynamics of racism in a world colored in many shades of gray resisted easy conclusions and drew all the viewers back into its intellectual and emotional complexity over and over. Everyone there found it easy to say, "Are you sure? I didn't see that in the film," as they challenged and re-educated each other.

The question, "Where did the film say that," gave them a textual focus outside themselves, objectifying the new information about racism and privilege as knowledge and experience "out there," and locating the impetus for change in the authority of the text rather than in a personal accusation of ignorance or prejudice by another. Returning to the text makes it safer, easier for students to hear that the old ideas are incomplete and that the new ideas are credible. Students are empowered to let go of the old and also to confront racist ideas, even from each other, with less worry about insulting or offending another person because the text is right there for them to use. I wish I had asked that question more often with Annabell's class and for all my students who need a pathway into a difficult conversation about race. In that spirit, I now offer the technique to readers for their own consideration and use in helping to change the world, one discussion moment at a time.

Even cognitively mature students like Annabell need specific instruction and mentorship in developing an anti-racist identity. In a racialized, racist society, even the most academically capable White students will often resist "new" information about racism that upends their world order. Their habit is frequently to rely on cautious analysis and demand more "facts" in the face of the illogic of normalized racist behavior or policy. First-year students are particularly vulnerable to confusion and being overwhelmed by the rapid flow of conflicting data and arguments and may back away from engagement and the call for social change. A teacher's recognition of and patience with the process of student development towards self-authorship can provide the student with both springboard and landing pad. With guidance, she can learn to ask incrementally, What does this text … the next class … the next experience have in the way of ideas I can use? With luck, she will find what she needs to venture out, keep looking and integrating new information to help her grow and speak out when needed. For others, like her friend Roberta in the next chapter, that process gets blocked and leaves her in a much less rewarding place.

Works Cited

Anderson, Elijah. *The Cosmopolitan Canopy: Race and Civility in Everyday Life*. W, W. Norton & Company, 2011.

Baxter Magolda, Marcia B. and Patricia M. King. *Learning Partnerships: Theory and Models of Practice to Educate for Self-Authorship*. Stylus, 2004.

Belenky, Mary Field et al. *Women's Ways of Knowing: The Development of Self, Voice and Mind*. 10th Anniversary Edition edition, HarperCollins Publishers, Inc. Basic Books, 1997.

Bolgatz, Jean. *Talking Race in the Classroom*. Teachers College Press, 2005.

Elias, Karen and Judith C. Jones. "Two Voices from the Front Lines: A Conversation About Race in the Classroom." *Race in the College Classroom: Pedagogy and Politics*, edited by Bonnie TuSmith and Maureen T. Reddy. Rutgers University Press, 2002, pp. 7–18.

Espinosa-Aguilar, Amanda. "Pretenders on the Throne: Gender, Race, and Authority in the Composition Classroom." *Calling Cards: Theory and Practice in the Study of Race, Gender, and Culture*, edited by Jacqueline Jones Royster and Ann Marie Mann Simpkins, State University of New York Press, 2005, pp. 147–157.

Fabiano, Patricia M. et al. "Engaging Men as Social Justice Allies in Ending Violence against Women: Evidence for a Social Norms Approach." *Journal of American College Health*, vol. 52.3, 2003, pp. 105–112.

Feagin, Joe R. *The White Racial Frame: Centuries of Racial Framing and Counter-Framing*. Routledge, 2010.

Fine, Michelle. "Witnessing Whiteness/Gathering Intelligence." *Off White: Readings on Power, Privilege, and Resistance*, edited by Michelle Fine et al., 2nd edition. Routledge, 2004, pp. 245–256.

George, Mark Patrick. "*Race Traitors, Exploring the Motivation and Action of White Antiracists*." Dissertation, University of New Mexico, 2004. Sociological Abstracts, CSA, Union Institute & University, doi:DA3129634 UMI, Ann Arbor, MI; 28 December 2005.

Helms, Janet E. "Toward a Model of White Racial Identity Development." *Black and White Racial Identity: Theory, Research, and Practice*, edited by Janet E. Helms. Praeger 1993, pp. 49–66.

Houts Picca, Leslie and Joe R. Feagin. *Two-Faced Racism: Whites in the Backstage and the Frontstage*. Routledge, 2007.

Lawrence, Sandra M. and Beverly Daniel Tatum. "White Educators as Allies: Moving from Awareness to Action." *Off White: Readings on Race, Privilege, and Resistance*, edited by Michelle Fine et al., 2nd edition. Routledge, 2004, pp. 362–372.

McIntosh, Peggy. "Examining Unearned Privilege." *Liberal Education*, vol. 79, no. 1, Winter 1993.

Ratcliffe, Krista. *Rhetorical Listening: Identification, Gender, Whiteness*. Southern Illinois University Press, 2005. *Studies in Rhetorics and Feminisms*, Shirley Glenn and Shirley Wilson Logan.

Sommers, Nancy and Laura Saltz. "The Novice as Expert: Writing the Freshman Year." *College Composition and Communication*, vol. 56, no. 1, 2004, pp. 124–149.

Trainor, Jennifer Seibel. *Rethinking Racism: Emotion, Persuasion, and Literacy Education in an All-White High School*. Southern Illinois University Press, 2008.

TuSmith, Bonnie. "Out on a Limb: Race and the Evaluation of Frontline Teaching." *Race in the College Classroom: Pedagogy and Politics*, edited by Bonnie TuSmith and Maureen T. Reddy. Rutgers University Press, 2002, pp. 112–125.

Watt, Sherry K. et al. "Privileged Identity Exploration: Examining Counselor Trainees' Reactions to Difficult Dialogues." *Counseling Education and Supervision*, vol. 49, 2009, pp. 86–105, Academic Search Premier.

· 4 ·

ROBERTA[1]

Critical compositionists have long struggled with the difficult dance between challenging students to growth and learning and scaring them into retreat, even resistance, to their curriculum. This delicate balance is particularly true when the curriculum involves themes related to identity-threatening issues such as race and racism, particularly for White students who, as mentioned earlier, may feel threatened, guilty, or in denial (Tatum 106). As the pedagogy has matured, critique and discussion of its goals and strategies has shifted from defense against charges of politics in the classroom (Hairston 698) and willful ignorance of students' pragmatic goals (Durst 111) to closer study of aspects of critical pedagogy in rhetoric. Key among these are feminist rhetorician Krista Ratcliffe's seminal analysis that essentially asks what resistance looks like in the classroom, generating a list of eight kinds of resistances that, she argued, students could learn to recognize in their responses so that they could get past them (138–139). A little later, Jennifer Seibol Trainor's composition study provided rich description of predominantly White suburban high school students resisting critical pedagogy to challenge the field to consider the role of

1. A version of this chapter was previously published as Lietz, Irene. "'When Do I Cross the Street?' Roberta's Guilty Reflection." *Journal of Expanded Perspectives on Learning* vol. 21, Winter 2015–2016, pp. 100–113.

their "emotioned" attachment to and investment in color-blindness and other aspects of the citizenship curriculum that is the cultural norm. Trainor uses the term "emotioned" to describe beliefs "that are not necessarily about race, per se ..." but are persuasive to students and people in general because of their integration in "routines and culture of schooling"; these beliefs are not logical but affective and "given force" by local, repeated experiences and feelings of (largely White) group identity (3).

This chapter is not an apology for critical pedagogy in composition. Instead, I would like to provide an application of the work of Ratcliffe and Trainor, but then begin to respond to some important next step questions. For me, after reading Ratcliffe and Trainor, the question remains: What do teachers *do* with student resistance? Should they just back away in deference to students' 'pragmatic goals' (Durst 111) and protests of discomfort? What are the ways that instructors can draw students through their resistance, help them get to the other side of cognitive dissonance (Harro 16), guilt (Tatum 105–113), and shame (Probyn) so that they can fully engage in a new critical understanding of the identity issues that shape and sometimes distort the rhetorical contexts and methods of their writing? Can a critical rhetoric of identity help students move past resistance to self-authorship (Baxter Magolda)?

In this chapter, I walk through the case study of another of my students, here named Roberta, that names her various triumphs and resistances, as Ratcliffe has defined them, while also considering their emotioned aspects, as described by Trainor's work. I also examine possible motives for her resistance, as theorized by Tatum and Harro. Finally, using Brown and Gilligan, Baxter Magolda, Winans, and Lu I discuss where the student's particular experience seems to fall short of a sense of accomplishment and identity resolution for her, including a self-critique of my version of the pedagogy at the time that points to some suggestions for strategies and institutional supports for teachers and students engaged in this kind of identity pedagogy.

Studying the interview responses of Roberta can contribute a case in point of the "local pedagogy" (Winans 256) of our particular campus, a small, predominantly female liberal arts university in southwestern Pennsylvania. Specifically, Roberta was a member of a race-themed writing class with Annabell that sought to teach the classic modes of writing combined with critical race theory to encourage students to make a personal connection to their mainly expository writing, and elevate it to higher levels of critical thinking, beyond the tired high-school level, talk-radio rhetoric about marijuana legalization, premarital sex, assisted suicide, and capital punishment.

While I seem to have more questions than answers about Roberta's experience of the class, the details of her story offer clues to understanding the sources of her fears and apparent self-censorship, as well as hints of the kind of support such students and their teachers need. Roberta's interviews also raise questions about what educators can fairly expect of or hope for students—and teachers—in a critical composition class. Ultimately, Roberta's story, as unresolved and unclear as it is at times, provides additional information about the struggles students experience in critical pedagogy, particularly in studying racial identity, and points to possible directions and questions for the future uses and study of this kind of learning and teaching experience.

Why Focus on Race in Particular?

To understand the context for Roberta's interviews, it's helpful to examine the rationale for doing this kind of class at all. This critical pedagogy focus grows out of the theory of Brazilian educator and philosopher Paulo Freire and his disciples. Using some of Freire's own words in the introduction to the foundational text, *Pedgagoy of the Oppressed*, American theologian Richard Shaull, a follower, writes that their liberatory work positions education as a vehicle to, "'the practice of freedom,' the means by which men and women deal critically and creatively with reality and discover how to participate in the transformation of their world" (qtd. in Freire 15). Later looking for ways to connect her rural students to their learning about the world, English professor Amy Winans found that studying race specifically "helps White students develop a personal investment in their work that serves as a basis for their thinking more critically about how race affects the lives of all people and how it structures the world in which they live" (255). Following up on similar studies of the effect of student diversity experiences described in Chapter 2, University of Iowa researchers found that diversity experiences promote significant gains in critical thinking, at least for White students. The effect for African American students was not as clear, perhaps due to the small size of the study samples (Pascarella et al. 257–259). In other words, studying race in a composition class can lead to meaningful and important effects in addition to learning to write.

The pedagogy of my class is built on the assumption that writing should not only prepare students for their subsequent writing experiences but also contribute in significant ways to students' growth and development as people.

To that end, though controversial, unpredictable, and complex, talking about race is intended to help students advance intellectually, socially, and emotionally, to ask "questions about race and racism, but, more important, to help others move beyond fear, beyond anger, beyond denial to new understanding of what racism is, how it impacts all of us, and ultimately what we can do about it" (Tatum ix). That requires courage, Tatum affirms, because a new understanding of racial identity inevitably upsets the old identity. Thus the resistance that others, including Krista Ratcliffe, Jennifer Seibol Trainor, Marlia Banning , Helen Fox , Pearl Rosenberg and more have also described in English, rhetoric, communication, teacher training, and other kinds of classes.

In other words, the worthiness of the outcomes still doesn't make it easy. Moreover, for a White woman raised in a White suburb who has come to an awareness of my own racial privilege relatively late in life, the race-themed composition class has pushed and pulled me into both identity and pedagogical adventures I did not anticipate. I believe many of the questions that Roberta's experience raises for me are both unique to my "positionality" as a White female teacher, to use a feminist research term (Rose), but also typical in some ways of the challenges faced by any well-intended teacher of critical pedagogy. That is the motivation for this chapter: to share what I have found but also to present the dilemmas we as individual teachers and members of the profession must confront and ultimately resolve if we hope to gain these ideal outcomes. I believe Roberta's journey has much to tell us.

Intellectually Excited But Emotionally, Morally Outraged

Roberta looked alive from the first moment of class. She engaged with everything, comfortably revealing her surprise at the idea that racism still exists. She readily confessed what she hadn't realized and didn't know, willing to take in new information if it was reasonable and evidenced. In fact, like her friend Annabell, it was the rational evidence that often carried the day with her; her emotions and passions followed, sometimes in spite of herself. Though the course was racially themed, its primary purpose was to teach first-year composition. This pedagogy is particularly well suited to helping students learn to state a thesis or judgment, identify appropriate support, and organize the argument suitably for a particular audience. All four students interviewed for this book, including Roberta, affirmed that the course helped them to build stronger arguments. Roberta named this process as critical thinking. She was intellectually stimulated by the course's expectation that she build an argument or "deeper conclusion" rather than "just facts." For example, to her profound surprise, the evidence of a racial bias in the sentencing guidelines for powder and crack cocaine led her to consider what other factors might maintain racism in the current legal system, but with a caveat that reveals her own bias:

> Even the fact that the crack-cocaine laws get such a harsher penalty than just powder cocaine, it doesn't necessarily mean that the people who made the laws were trying to be racist. They probably just viewed it as such a more dangerous drug, and that's why they did that. But the fact that there's such a racial disparity in the people being prosecuted and stuff, and that that's just getting ignored, even after multiple recommendations from the United States Sentencing Commission, and other various groups. I guess that that's what I found was the racist part of it.

Roberta found the evidence so compelling in itself and the authority of the U.S. Sentencing Commission so obviously persuasive to a reasonable person that she felt forced to conclude that people who are maintaining the current guidelines are operating out of racism rather than an exculpating lack of information. But here is the rub: her excuses for the responsible lawmakers as operating out of concern for the greater danger of the drug indicates the kind of denial that Ratcliffe references:

> *Denial* emerges when students or teachers refuse to acknowledge the existence of an idea or action. Denial also emerges when students or teachers acknowledge the existence of an idea or action but refuse to acknowledge any accountability—individual and/or systemic—for any privileges or obstacles afforded us by (the history of) this idea or action. (138)

Researchers found this same denial in an inter-university study of Master's in Counseling students who "expressed thoughts that argued against the anxiety provoked during discussions regarding racism, heterosexism/homophobia, and ableism by stating that those injustices did not exist" (Watt et al. 96). Roberta's response also rings of "deflection," that is shifting "the focus … toward less threatening targets, such as a parent or the school system" (Watt et al. 98). Exactly what threat was she experiencing? It seems to be the threat of needing to put less trust in the people in charge, realizing the kind of authority she had so long trusted may not be trustworthy in their reactions to the known injustice of the disparate sentencing.

Roberta was caught in a classic clash among conflicting sources. Like all of us, as described by long-time social justice educators Rita Hardiman, Bailey Jackson, and Pat Griffin, Roberta "had learned to accept systems of oppression as normal through interactions with parents, peers, teachers, and other influential individuals"(40). Hardiman and associates also note that oppression is taught "through experiences in schools, religious organizations, and our encounters with health care, criminal justice systems, and other institutions that affect our daily lives" (40). When this socialization, along with the strong ethical/moral training she had also received was brought into proximity with the factual evidence of defacto racism in the disparate drug penalties, she faced a crisis. Her resulting cognitive dissonance carried her swiftly into denial that the lawmakers' failure to fix the sentencing guidelines could be anything but innocent or even civic-minded. Why?

As education professors Anne Laughlin and Elizabeth Creamer have found, students who are early in their academic career and/or self-authorship journey rely on personal relationships and "societal expectations" (48) rather than on thorough consideration of multiple, alternative perspectives, "thereby reinforcing their dependence on external authority" (50). White first-year students like Roberta generally do not have much practice with the complexities of being challenged in their racial identity, and find it disconcerting to realize that the authorities they have always trusted—parents, peers, school, church—have intentionally or unintentionally misled them in the reasons for institutionally racist policies.

In addition to a developmental slope in attachment to authority, Baxter Magolda's longitudinal study illustrates the connection between students' self-authorship and the developmental time needed for them to incorporate emotioned learning as well as intellect. As one of her study subjects explained,

> In the college classroom there is a focus on intellect and not necessarily the feel of what is going on. It is a much more controlled environment. What you learn after college is how out of control the environment is. Life is about dealing with those particular out-of-control situations. (70)

In other words, while a rhetorical recognition of denial as a kind of resistance to critical pedagogy is helpful, adding an interdisciplinary dip into student development theory on self-authorship helps characterize Roberta's ready absolution of the legislators as a call for patience with students' developmental stages. Seeing Roberta's denial through a self-authorship lens also shifts at least some of the responsibility from her shoulders to the teacher and the curriculum. Trainor's work, discussed later in this chapter, points to deficiencies in our understanding of and approaches to the emotioned gaps engendered in our school systems. Baxter Magolda's work addresses pedagogical innovations to link self-authorship directly and pragmatically with the kinds of rhetorical outcomes we intend for Roberta and her classmates.

From a psychological perspective, Lyn Mikel Brown and Carol Gilligan contend a person's unwillingness to hold accountable those in whom she has placed trust may be because such action may conflict with the self-image she is cultivating. Brown and Gilligan described this dilemma in the case of their research subject "Neeti," who sought to develop "a conventional, authoritative voice ... modeling herself on the image of the perfectly nice and caring girl" (39). Perhaps the interviews reveal this 'nice girl' side of Roberta when she couldn't dare to believe that the lawmakers might have deliberately crafted a law with racist effect; such awareness on her part would open a Pandora's box of other conflicts for her, even as she most likely struggled with a myriad of other first-year college student identity issues. Instead some students, and I include Roberta in this group, choose instead to silence themselves, to modulate their voices, as Neeti had, and "muffle" their resistance:

> We know that women in particular, often speak in indirect discourse, in voices deeply encoded, deliberately or unwittingly opaque. As White heterosexual women living in the context of twentieth-century North America--as women whose families in childhood were working-class and Jewish, respectively--we know from our own experience about certain strategies of resistance, both the danger of an outspoken political resistance and the corrosive suffering of psychological resistance. (24)

Though Roberta appeared to me, her teacher, to cope with the vicissitudes and vagaries of the race-themed course better than many of her peers, her resistance, even as benign as it might appear in her essay and in class discussion, signals a struggle with the concepts of the course and their inherent challenges to the adult identity she was developing.

When Roberta spoke to me about the lawmakers' rejection of the Sentencing Commission's recommendation to fix the disparate drug penalties for crack and powder cocaine, her voice rose with emotion. She was angry that they were falling short of her ethical standard, when even she, a first-year student, could see the injustice of the status quo. Probyn's work on shame and writing offers another possible insight to Roberta's confusing resistance to the call for action inherent in the class pedagogy. Perhaps Roberta's passion for justice sets up her later shame about her expressed inability to do more than put words to paper about it, as I will discuss later. Probyn comments on a different shaming situation with similarities to Roberta's case, one in which writers fear being exposed as incompetent or a sham:

> The crucial element that turns sham into shame is the level of interest and desire involved. There is no shame in being a sham if you don't care what others think or if you don't care what you think. But if you do, shame threatens. To care intensely about what you are writing places the body within the ambit of the shameful: sheer disappointment in the self amplifies to a painful level. (131)

Roberta's strong orientation to justice was expressed in her commitment to a theology major, so the intellectual puzzle of how lawmakers could resist evidence of racial disparity also spoke to her sense of moral (dis)order. Gesturing in frustration, she questioned the opaque logic of their actions. In other words, she had all the precursors to feeling like a sham and experiencing shame at her later inability to take more definite action towards implementing social justice change.

The Personal Is Political

As Roberta reflected on her growth in her writing and understanding of racism, she displayed admirable courage in moving from the romanticism of brainy, provocative research and logic that appealed to her sense of justice to amazingly open and honest critical analysis of her own life, including the personal pain of acknowledging her own possible racism. She bravely narrated just such an experience in a frank story about walking down the street at night as an African American approached and the resulting internal debate about whether or not it is racist to cross to the other side:

> One of the examples that I was thinking about, was, If I'm walking down the sidewalk, and there's someone walking towards me, what differs in the fact that I don't feel safe? [I]f it's a White man walking towards me – if it's an adult male – he's bigger than I am, no matter what. If he had some sort of bad intentions, you know, he could still easily overpower me. And, so could a Black man walking towards me. But, when do I cross the street? Do I cross the street for both of them because I don't trust them just because they could overpower me, or is it because it's a Black man? Does that make him more subject to causing the crime? That's what I realized: just because he's walking down the street. He could just be just on his way to doing something whatever, like going to the gym. Who knows? He's not doing anything bad, but in the back

> of my mind you still kind of think that, that maybe I trust him less than I would trust a White man. And that's just not fair to think that way at all.

Although any woman, regardless of her race, might express fear in a similar situation, Roberta suspected that at least some of her concern was based on racial criteria, whether she wanted that to be part of her psyche or not. So she was also afraid of the racism she had acquired. Her fear that her Whiteness was misleading her, trapping her, may be key to understanding her ultimate hesitance, discussed later, to feel capable of taking more definite steps toward an active anti-racism commitment as part of her own racial identity.

Reminiscent of Annabell's comment, Roberta also somewhat shamefacedly confessed her own fear of difference when she revealed that the Whiteness of her teacher (me, in this case) contributed to her sense of safety in telling that story on herself. She feared being misunderstood and committing a social faux pas, attesting to the phenomenon that Espinosa-Aguilar notes in her analysis of student resistance, that "students may not believe that our contestatory classrooms are truly safe environments for the expression of their views" (Espinosa-Aguilar 155). On the other hand, other researchers have noted that students "often mention that the homogeneity [of some all-White classes] makes it easier for them to talk openly about race" (Winans 260). As a White student with a White teacher in the privacy of my office, Roberta felt safe enough to admit that she questioned her own sincerity and ability to live with integrity as a racially aware person, even as she later argued the necessity of her generation taking up the anti-racist torch.

Ultimately, in her first-year interview, Roberta admitted that while the course "opened my eyes to a lot of things," she also felt "I'm just one person and that I can't have an effect." But then she went on to give a rational response to herself: "You know that's not true. I vote, you know, and I'm just one vote. And if I thought it didn't have an effect, why would I even go to the polls to vote?" But her commitment seemed hesitant, perhaps something she wished she could believe when she said, "I don't know what I would do to stop it [racism] other than to stop it in my life and have that be, like, an example to others." Then she backed away almost entirely, referring to my teaching about racism: "But to take such an active role as you are, it just seems like would be overwhelming. It seems really ideal to want to do something to stop it but I don't think I could live in the Cultural House." The Cultural House is a nearby university living option open to all students that the class visited for an interracial dialogue experience. Roberta explained how she didn't believe she could sustain such attention to race and racism beyond our class experience, such as living at the Cultural House: "Just having to deal with it all the time, I guess, having to think about it all the time. I don't know, maybe … I'm not sure. I don't know if I would pursue racism education further. Not that I didn't think it was interesting, but …" Then she stopped talking, waiting for another question from me, the interviewer.

At that moment at the end of her first year, Roberta looked burned out and defeated, confessing she was glad to be done with the course and its topic. I had hoped when we met again to talk in her senior year that she might have resolved some of her dilemma and perhaps found other support for doing what she felt was important but could not muster the ongoing energy for. In other words, I was looking for some confirmation that the experience of researching and writing the facts about race could help move students from being a bystander to being an agent of social justice change, as all good critical pedagogy intends. But the picture in her senior year was very mixed: while different somewhat, also much the same as in her first year.

The Cost of Inexperience That Gets No Institutional Support

In that senior interview, Roberta said she felt she had changed over the course of college, that through our first-year class, some women's studies classes, and her theology major she had acquired new understanding of oppression and prejudice. But she had not returned to the topic of race very much for the rest of her college career. She noted the silence in the curriculum about race at our university, saying that if a student didn't want to talk about race, she could avoid it easily.

As at many predominantly White schools, she noted no hostility on campus but that there was a level of racial segregation; it was much easier for the Black and White students to sit separately in the cafeteria. She wasn't sure she would feel welcome at the Black students' table, although we didn't talk about testing that reality. Admittedly, it was not her fault that the curriculum or co-curricular experiences apparently did not engage her in further racial identity development, but she seemed relieved that no one challenged her insularity.

Having moved off-campus after her first year, she found more racial "intermingling" as she called it in the neighborhoods in the university district and the east side of the city where many students lived. She had observed differences in the way the police treated student parties, noting how they "busted" two Black guys for being "troublemakers" but only confiscated beers from the White underage girls, telling them to turn down their music, and sending them home without any arrests. She relayed these stories with a knowing, resigned air, as if she had traveled a long way from her own pre-college White suburban experience in which she had trusted the police to be unbiased.

Roberta's critical awareness was strong enough to make her question her own assumptions, though she couldn't always resolve the conflicts. In her senior interview as she talked about whether she noticed race in her life, she told a story about how her Asian co-workers at a local restaurant reacted to her long-time Black friend:

> When it comes to people when I hang out at work, I definitely notice our cultural differences a lot more. A lot of them were born in Indonesia or Burma. They have a lot of different ways of doing things. I'm always surprised like sometimes even they will say something. My one friend who is a Black guy, he lived next door in my junior year and then he moved a block away and so we hang out all the time. He came into the restaurant one day and they all said, "Why are you hanging out with a Black guy?" I don't know. I didn't think of it that way because we have a lot in common: he listens to the same kind of music and he's really good friends with my roommate too. So I don't know. Sometimes I can notice the difference really easily and sometimes it's not a thing at all. Maybe it's because I've only been working for 8 months so that's kinda new and he's a friend that I've had for three years now. I have a more comfortable relationship with him but sometimes [race is] more noticeable than others.

Roberta's story exemplifies a person in the process of changing her social identity. With interesting complexity, she was clearly aware of the racism in her co-workers' reaction to her friend. But she hadn't noticed the assumption in her words that "even they will say something," as if members of all minority groups were homogenous in their racial awareness. Her co-workers' challenge to her relationship with her Black friend apparently triggered a subconscious insecurity: she questioned her own motives and defended the friendship as color-blind. Even as she relayed the story, though, she seemed to be suspicious of herself and her feelings, wanting to dismiss race as a factor in their friendship but aware of feeling social pressures to be simultaneously color-blind and yet critically aware.

She insisted that she had changed since our first-year class, noting her efforts and duty to see "the absolute value and dignity of each human life. As a White person, I'm trying to see that in everybody." She defined her identity in terms of personal action, saying, the class "has made me identify racism, acknowledge it, which changes it. Being around difference has changed me." She confessed,

> Even though I don't want racial thoughts, I still have stereotypes. The more I know, the more I can stop myself and try to make a difference. Eventually it will be my generation in charge. No good comes from blindness. Maybe you're not personally doing it, but we need to change the institutionalized racism. Our generation is a lot farther along but that doesn't mean all is fine. If it's part of society, we have to acknowledge it.

In other words, action was part of her credo, but as she said that, I wondered if being an astute observer of racial inequity sufficiently met her criterion for action in her mind.

Roberta epitomized for me the White student—or teacher—who believes it important to call out racism when she sees it and to name the evil among us so that we have some hope of someday eliminating it. Yet she seemed to be treading water in the same racial identity place she described in her first year, that is she could not imagine herself acting against racism in any public way. If her major in theology did not expressly require a class that examined some aspect of racism, then she felt no compulsion to seek out ways to respond to the institutionalized racism that she was still confident existed: "It just didn't come up. I didn't get to take much outside of my major. My history class was of dystopia and utopias, so it wasn't actual history. So that also depends if I'd taken regular history like the civil war and race relations." And though in her senior year interview, she said that her racial attitudes had profoundly changed and that the class had impacted her life in a major way, (although her concept of "history" still seems somewhat conventionally narrow), she apparently felt no more prepared than in her first-year interview to take action on her new-found attitudes. She almost shrugged her shoulders at me, as if the matter were out of her hands.

In many ways, Roberta had seemed primed and ready, at the edge of an active commitment: when presented with the fork in the road between choices identified by social justice educator Bobbie Harro "Change, raise consciousness, interrupt, educate, take a stand, question, reframe," and the alternative "Do nothing, don't make waves, promote the status quo" (16), Roberta seemed ready to move in the direction of change. But she didn't feel she could go there, and I continue to wonder why.

The Emotioned Gap

Without being overly critical of either Roberta or myself, I now believe that she and I, as well as the rest of the White people in the class, were caught in the gap between what we came to see as a necessary revision of our White identities and our emotional attachment to our past image of ourselves. White people want to see themselves as innocent of the taint of racism as good, well-intentioned people. At the same time, they want (need) to stay attached to families, friends, neighbors, schools, churches, communities, and institutions that maintain their White privilege, even as they want to abandon White privilege. Intellectually they've made the shift but emotionally they have not, leaving them guilty and conflicted.

On this point, there is much to learn from composition professor Jennifer Seibol Trainor's study of students in an all-White high school English class. Trainor might point out that my course focused on the logos of composition and racism in U.S. society but did not address the gap between the intellectual complexity of what we were studying and the pathos of simplistic dictums for the value of hard work and a positive attitude. She describes this dilemma so vividly: Students' emotional attachment to the hidden curriculum of good citizenship, independent achievement, hard work, stiff-lipped perseverance over adversity, equal opportunity, and deliberate color-blindness to avoid any hint of racist preference. This narrative, she argues, is often reinforced by teachers' unwillingness to confront directly the dominant narrative as incomplete and limiting, which reinforces that difference and critical thinking are alien values that threaten our way of life and the happiness and harmony of our communities. Trainor generalizes this experience in our high schools, a claim that my students' early responses to the race-themed curriculum would bear out. Their responses are almost uniform as they talk about how they were taught to avoid noticing color and that, while there were social cliques, everyone was treated equally, including the occasional student of color who was almost always a standout athlete, well-liked and widely accepted.

Roberta's high school experience in a suburb of Cleveland was no different. So it could be that Roberta's struggle with the gap between her expressed belief in racial equality but her fatigue in examining lived race critically was a form of fallout from courses like ours that do not directly help students cope with the emotioned gap between their carefully constructed color-blind identities and conflicting information from Others' lived experience. Educators need to work harder to bring together the intellectual and emotional experiences engendered in writing classes, particularly when critical pedagogy successfully brings students to new awareness that demands some public remedy on the part of members of the dominant groups.

But that leaves many questions unanswered. Roberta had "challenged the essentialized notions of identity that are often caught in the dichotomy of innocence and guilt," as Winans calls for our pedagogies to enable (Winans 258). Roberta knew she was basically a moral person who could also fall into stereotypical thinking as a result of the "smog" of racism in our society, as she was aware that Tatum describes negative cultural influences (6). She knew her classmates were seeing the world too narrowly when they provided their interracial friendships as evidence of their own lack of bias. She did not flinch at the questions posed by her Asian co-workers that challenged her own long-time friendship with a Black man. And she readily recognized her potential privilege in the differential treatment received by other partying White students given police reprieves that nearby Black students did not enjoy. Her worldview was complicated and nuanced, which should have helped her navigate the treacherous waters of the guilt/innocence dichotomy. But the evidence of her interviews would suggest that a student's intellectually nuanced view, and pedagogical strategies that recognize the emotional and other legacies of racism in our schools, as laudable as they are, do not take us far enough yet.

By distancing herself from the reactions of her classmates, Roberta tried to establish repeatedly that she was not racist, that she was a good White person. But then, what is a good White person? Is thinking differently enough? At what point does thinking need to commit externally to some action, such as the interruption of jokes in the "backstage" of same-race groups, as sociologists Houts Picca and Feagin have described and as her friend Annabell has done. Isn't it necessary, as English professors Lu and Horner conclude, that "we can use experience to not simply affirm our state of being but to raise questions about that material being, to critique and bring about changes in the conditions of our existence, and in turn, to transform our experience" (261)? Roberta seemed to have difficulty moving beyond her particular material experience to "politicize" it, as Lu and Horner call for, as a way to make it transformative (261). In another article, Lu refers to Anzaldua's metaphorical "borderlands," the potentially transformative space between the known and the new world or knowledge, where static awareness can move to a more active consciousness: the painful struggle to birth new understanding "enables a border resident to act on rather than merely react to the conditions of her or his life, turning awareness of the situation into 'inner changes' which in turn bring about 'changes in society'" (Lu "Conflict" 888). But Roberta claimed that this kind of movement from the personal to public action was "too overwhelming," a position too hard to sustain, which left her caught between the rock of racism and the hard place of an activist anti-racist White identity.

Perhaps in trying to establish a place for herself in academic discourse, Roberta may have also fallen into the gap between home/society, her past experiences in talking about race through the lens of color-blindness, and the pressure of the class to adopt an anti-racist identity. This identity conflict is similar to that again described by Lu, in which she tried to reconcile the conflicting discourses of her progressive and Western-educated home with the contrasting worker identity of 1950s revolutionary China, as taught in her school ("From Silence" 445), a conflict that ultimately silenced her. As a result, Lu struggled in her reading and writing, believing that she was supposed to keep her two worlds discrete, an impossible task as she strove to establish a unified identity for herself. In this same article, she later explained how she might have worked her way between the two conflicting discourses to a stance of her own, but could only do that with more study and more exposure to other voices that could show her how to negotiate this new identity.

Roberta did not have the advantage of additional study in writing or talking about race. She did not find allies, models, or mentors in our class or in the rest of her college experience. Like the others in this study, Roberta reported very little additional experience in racial dialogue beyond our class. This shortfall is in no way her fault, but a failure on the part of my curriculum perhaps, and even more I believe, our university, as discussed further a little later.

Remaining Tensions

The unfinished and incomplete nags me, and, I contend, other White students like Roberta who accept the challenge of engaging with an anti-racist critical pedagogy but find it hard to commit to activism. In addition to the emotioned and intellectual gaps discussed earlier, there are so many unfinished thoughts and loose ends in this kind of course-based project. What does one do, for example, with the residuals of having been raised White in a world that privileges White? When prejudiced thoughts emerge unbidden and uncontrolled, how does a White person—student or teacher—continue to justify herself without some accountability for her racist thoughts, in spite of herself? By the end of the course, it was clear to Roberta that there was more work to be done; the disappointment of the course for both of us was that she did not see a way for her to sustain herself in that work. What's more, at this point in my evaluation of this project, I believe it is naive to expect to make greater progress in a single semester, especially in a first-year course.

Perhaps that is a harsh evaluation of what we were involved in. Granted, educators deserve credit for having conversations and exploring territory that the majority of White America avoids. But it's hard to find the line of "well done" or "good enough" when the African American students who have been involved in such courses are clearly more inclined to respond, "Really?" After all, how long can people of color wait for White people to figure this out? The costs of not figuring this out are enormous, overwhelming, and unacceptable.

In response to those who maintain this work is too hard or too political, particularly for first-year students, I ask: even if it is an unfinished product, if teachers can guide these students with disciplinary integrity in a process of learning to write in ways that bring them to greater relationship with others different from themselves while increasing their own self-awareness and voice, shouldn't they? If this kind of course can be a vehicle of social change or greater civil engagement, shouldn't it be? In fact, without obligating every teacher to be a critical teacher, don't people agree that we have a responsibility to open pathways for our students towards greater skill *and* personal competency, whatever the pedagogy or methodology?

To me, Roberta's story demonstrates several things. Using a race-themed pedagogy does indeed prompt growth in writing and critical thinking, as well as deep student engagement in real-world issues that impact students' personal and professional lives. It is not without its complications or unresolved questions. For example, what are we to do when even the best students and teachers who are honestly struggling to create change are unable to sustain an anti-racist project longer than one sixteen-week course? What obligation does the (White) student (or the White teacher) have to recognize the need to act for the sake of greater justice? What level of accountability do educators hold for student outcomes that do not result in revised world views of their privilege? How do teachers respect White students' developmental pace of learning and their free choice to be who they believe they should be, but also lead, encourage, support, and even prod them into action, and help them move beyond perpetual guilt?

Even further, I believe the even more pressing questions lie within education's institutional structures. How can the institutions of higher education claim to prepare students to live competently in an increasingly diverse society yet leave students and teachers to struggle in isolated, one-shot, short-term experiences that have little hope of a satisfactory or effective end? Especially among those schools that profess social justice and civic engagement as desirable core curriculum outcomes, how is it ethical to leave students (or teachers) hanging untethered, blowing in the wind, without mechanisms of support, such as scaffolded diversity experiences, robust diversity in student enrollment and faculty employment, more substantial dialogue on campuses among speakers and topics that challenge privilege, particularly White privilege, more courageous institutional self-assessment of assumptions, assignments, policies and procedures that effect defacto racism, and more?

The difficulties that Roberta faced are symptomatic not only of her courageous battle with White socialization but provide a clarion call for education to do better by her and all of our students, as well as by her teachers who are currently operating largely in isolation.

Teachers cannot and should not back down when they encounter resistance from students because it is merely a reflection of the work they have yet to do. I am grateful for the Robertas of our world who are willing to learn with us and grateful for this professional community who believe in the importance of integrity in this work. And I continue to hope that as we come to understand the kinds of responses we get from our students, we, as a profession, can eventually puzzle this out in more complete and satisfactory ways.

What I Wish I Had Said

I now understand that Roberta was experiencing several kinds of cognitive dissonance that I could have helped her negotiate in several specific ways. The previous pages have illustrated her struggle with (1) a disabling separation of logic and emotion; (2) how to dig more deeply into the data, text, or experience to understand complex, nuanced evidence; (3) inexperience in critical analysis of racially inflected situations; (4) a lack of anti-racist models. I wish I had offered her the following ideas and experiences.

First, Roberta, like her friend Annabell, was very logic-oriented and had learned very well to separate reasoning from emotion as much of traditional schooling teaches. Her study of theology in a predominantly female university seems to have educated her, to use Belenky and associates' terms, in a mix of "separate knowing," more typical of males who are oriented toward external, impersonal rules (101), and "connected knowing," a common female orientation, that requires more than just facts but opportunity to develop empathy with the details of others' lives (115). Perhaps for Roberta, the "separate knowing" was more primary as she problematically separated emotion from logic.

Trainor's work includes consideration of scholars who have studied the strong links between emotion and learning, including the fundamental idea that emotion is not separate from reason, particularly moral reasoning (21–22), which was probably the focus of Roberta's theology classes. Roberta's strong intellectual/moral reasoning skills could have been better supported in our class with more Socratic questioning that helped her uncover the emotionally-inflected disinformation she had absorbed. For example, we could have spent more class time exploring the sources of White fear of people of color, particularly the stereotype of the oversexed, criminally prone Black male. In Roberta's thought experiment about when she would cross the street as a man approached her, she felt guilty at responding more fearfully to the Black man than the White man without reference to the fearful, racist all-White environment in which she was raised or the continued pervasiveness of the stereotype in society generally. This unexamined "separate knowing" left her carrying all the blame for something that was not her fault. Students need help to learn to examine critically the emotional sources of their beliefs.

Second, to strengthen Roberta's skills in critical analysis related to race, the class could have also emphasized the use of the question, "Has anyone seen any (more) data related to that idea or situation?" This question might have helped Roberta see that she had stopped her thinking about race before she was done, probably for the variety of reasons discussed in this and other chapters. The additional data she needed to help resolve her stasis and guilt might have come from her own or others' research, but it could also have taken the form of some "connected learning," as Belenky, et al. have termed it. Connected knowing, that is knowledge of people and emotion, provides a pathway from intellect to "commitment; it is something to live by" (149).

To provide this connected knowing, other anti-racist educators use the social justice project associated with critical race classes. Early in my own anti-racist teaching, I encountered the work of Helen Fox who suggests a variety of creative and classroom-tested projects that her students (and mine, subsequently) have found helpful as an application of their learning (Fox 109–186). For example, in later classes my students offered mini seminars to other students outside of the class to raise awareness of common racist stereotypes. Others interviewed students who were not in the class to uncover their encounters with campus racism. These kinds of student-generated experiences provide qualitative data that validate students' understanding of racism in their lives, moving them beyond cognitive dissonance and despair to a sense of empowerment to act as part of an anti-racist community, whether local or universal.

Third, Roberta felt the need to apply her new knowledge of how race works in the world but felt unsuccessful in her attempt. To acquire adult experience, she chose to move out of the dorm and into the very diverse student neighborhoods in the university district. Some of her story in this chapter includes references to new insights about herself and Others, but also how her unaccompanied independent thinking, without benefit of a class context, seemed unable to carry her to "connected knowing." It may have been helpful for her to have additional opportunities either in my class or others to examine critically those experiences further, learning to apply the facts that she was learning to the emotions that she was experiencing. But that experience came later in her college career when, she contends, she had no further opportunities to discuss race and racism in the context of a college class to support further critical skill development. This timing was a sadly missed opportunity for Roberta that I hope she found a way to remedy later.

Fourth, students like Roberta appreciate models to help them to visualize a goal. Fox also suggests more direct teaching of historical models of White allies, such as Viola Liuzzo, James Reeb, or Michael Schwerner from the Civil Rights Movement of the 1960s; Fr. William Cunningham and Eleanor Josaitis who founded Focus Hope in Detroit after the 1967 uprising; Morris Dees, the founder of the Southern Poverty Law Center, and many more. Such study provides a counter narrative to the disillusion and overwhelming helplessness that sometimes accompanies new awareness of pervasive racism. Knowing the stories of White allies also gives students like Roberta permission or personal authority as a White person to confront problems accompanied by a sense of a community of support. With such models, students can begin to see the possibility of a positive White identity, instead of feeling helpless, hopeless, and overwhelmed by the immensity of the problem of racism.

My strong sense is that with more time immersed in the subject of racism with more guidance, Roberta could have moved beyond her despair and inaction. She could have been shown how to accept imperfection in the authority figures she trusted and in herself as an imperfect seeker of truth, without compromising her principles of equity and humanity. Although I should have found ways to offer her more support, no teacher can do it all for every student.

That conundrum points directly to the need for further integration of critical anti-racist study throughout the curriculum. But this kind of curricular reform is an institutional responsibility, as are the teacher and student support systems, attention to diverse student and faculty recruitment and sustainability, and institutional climate and policy review and monitoring that are components of a cultural "cosmopolitan canopy" (Anderson), as mentioned in Annabell's chapter, to nurture and support racially healthy educational environments and workplaces.

A more integrated approach to critical race study throughout the campus, with time to process some hands-on experience with difference, could have added much to Roberta's understanding of herself and those around her. But the classroom and the teacher must also be prepared to deal with the fast-changing panorama of emotion that plays such havoc with student experiences. In the next chapter, Elaine's story chronicles her difficulty—and mine—when the classroom study of racism becomes a site of very confusing emotion.

Works Cited

Anderson, Elijah. *The Cosmopolitan Canopy: Race and Civility in Everyday Life*. W.W. Norton & Company, 2011.

Banning, Marlia E. "The Politics of Resentment." *JAC*, vol. 26, no. 1–2, 2006, pp. 65–101.

Baxter Magolda, Marcia B. "Self-Authorship: The Foundation for Twenty-First-Century Education." *New Directions for Teaching and Learning*, edited by Peggy S. Meszaros, vol. 109. Wiley InterScience, 2007, pp. 69–83. Academic Search Premier.

Belenky, Mary Field et al. *Women's Ways of Knowing: The Development of Self, Voice and Mind*. 10th Anniversary Edition edition, HarperCollins Publishers, Inc. Basic Books, 1997.

Brown, Lyn Mikel and Carol Gilligan. *Meeting at the Crossroads: Women's Psychology and Girls' Development*. Ballantine Books, 1992.

Durst, Russel K. "Can We Be Critical of Critical Pedagogy?" *College Composition and Communication*, vol. 58, no. 1, 2006, pp. 110–113.

Espinosa-Aguilar, Amanda. "Pretenders on the Throne: Gender, Race, and Authority in the Composition Classroom." *Calling Cards: Theory and Practice in the Study of Race, Gender, and Culture*, edited by Jacqueline Jones Royster and Ann Marie Mann Simpkins. State University of New York Press, 2005, pp. 147–157.

Fox, Helen. *"When Race Breaks Out": Conversations About Race and Racism in College Classrooms*. vol. 6. Peter Lang, 2004. *Questions About the Purpose(S) of Colleges & Universities*, Norm Denizen, Josef Progler, Joe L. Kincheloe, Shirley R. Steinberg.

Freire, Paulo. *Pedagogy of the Oppressed*. translated by Myra Bergman Ramos. Continuum, 1983.

Hairston, Maxine. "Diversity, Ideology, and Teaching Writing." *Cross-Talk in Comp Theory: A Reader*, edited by Victor Villanueva, 2nd edition. NCTE, 1992, pp. 697–713.

Hardiman, Rita et al. "Conceptual Foundations for Social Justice Education." *Teaching for Diversity and Social Justice*, edited by Maurianne Adams et al., 2nd edition. Routledge, 2007, pp. 35–66.

Harro, Bobbie. "The Cycle of Socialization." *Readings for Diversity and Social Justice*, edited by Maurianne Adams et al.. Routledge, 2000, pp. 15–21.

Houts Picca, Leslie and Joe R. Feagin. *Two-Faced Racism: Whites in the Backstage and the Frontstage*. Routledge, 2007.

Laughlin, Anne and Elizabeth G. Creamer. "Engaging Differences: Self-Authorship and the Decision-Making Process." *New Directions for Teaching and Learning*, vol. 109, 2007, pp. 43–51. Wiley InterScience, doi:10.1002/tl.264.

Lu, Min-Zhan. "Conflict and Struggle: The Enemies or Preconditions of Basic Writing?" *College English*, vol. 54, no. 8, 1992, pp. 887–913, JSTOR.

—. "From Silence to Words: Writing as Struggle." *College English*, vol. 49, no. 4, 1987, pp. 437–448, JSTOR.

Lu, Min-Zhan and Bruce Horner. "The Problematic of Experience: Redefining Critical Work in Ethnography and Pedagogy." *College English*, vol. 60, no. 3, 1998, pp. 257–277, JSTOR.

Pascarella, Ernest T. et al. "Do Diversity Experiences Influence the Development of Critical Thinking?" *Journal of College Student Development*, vol. 42, no. 3, 2001, pp. 257–271, ProQuest.

Probyn, Elspeth. *Blush: The Face of Shame*. University of Minnesota Press, 2005.

Ratcliffe, Krista. *Rhetorical Listening: Identification, Gender, Whiteness*. Southern Illinois University Press, 2005. *Studies in Rhetorics and Feminisms*, Shirley Glenn and Shirley Wilson Logan.

Rose, Damaris. *Revisiting Feminist Research Methodologies: A Working Paper*. edited by Research Division Status of Women Canada, 2001. 20 June 2007.

Rosenberg, Pearl M. "Color Blindness in Teacher Education: An Optical Delusion." *Off White: Readings on Power, Privilege, and Resistance*, edited by Michelle Fine et al., 2nd edition. Routledge, 2004, pp. 257–272.

Tatum, Beverly Daniel. *"Why Are All the Black Kids Sitting Together in the Cafeteria?" And Other Conversations About Race*. Basic Books, 2003.

Trainor, Jennifer Seibel. *Rethinking Racism: Emotion, Persuasion, and Literacy Education in an All-White High School.* Southern Illinois University Press, 2008.

Watt, Sherry K. et al. "Privileged Identity Exploration: Examining Counselor Trainees' Reactions to Difficult Dialogues." *Counseling Education and Supervision*, vol. 49, 2009, pp. 86–105, Academic Search Premier.

Winans, Amy E. "Local Pedagogies and Race: Interrogating White Safety in the Rural College Classroom." *College English*, vol. 67, no. 3, 2005, pp. 253–273, JSTOR.

· 5 ·

ELAINE[1]

The fear in Elaine's eyes seemed to magnify their whites, yet there was a perpetual smile on her lips as she sat in the chair next to my desk in the privacy of my office. She clearly did not want to alienate me with her harsh words but she seemed oblivious to the presence of an African American administrative assistant sitting just outside the door. She seemed to feel driven to make her point; I wasn't understanding *her* life experience. She conjured pictures of the idyllic farm and small-town high school within an hour of our urban institution. She laughed deprecatingly but also lovingly about "tractor day" just before prom when the boys wore their big buckled belts, jeans, and cowboy shirts while the girls rode at their sides, parading their fathers' farm machinery around the school parking lot and into town. She wanted to know, what did any of this talk about racism have to do with the essays we were writing in our first-year composition class? Why couldn't we all just get along and stop talking about race? It only made things worse between the "colored" people and the rest of us. She also told of the fear she felt on the city bus that she

1. A version of this chapter was previously published as Lietz, Irene. "'Anyone Can Hurt You': Elaine's Attack and Defense in Writing About Race." *Language Arts Journal of Michigan* vol. 28, no. 2, Spring 2013, pp. 47–54.

perceived as filled with Black people who regarded her and her boyfriend with fear and suspicion as she clutched his arm.

Where does this fear come from? How does it work? What could I understand that would help students respond to this fear in a constructive manner so that they can get past their fear and learn something new, without triggering other fears or defensive reactions in the rest of the students or in me? Fear and its responses, including both attack and defense, are on the continuum of student responses to critical race pedagogy, which teachers need to recognize, understand their sources, and find ways to incorporate their constituent resistance into the learning experience. In the next few pages, I will describe Elaine, one particularly fearful student, and the context for understanding the sources and dynamics of this fear. In Elaine's case, her response was a complex mixture of desire to be seen as a good person overlaid with a strong fear that her own identity and her understanding of her family, her friends and neighbors, virtually her entire world might not survive the prospective learning experience. From such a stance, it is no wonder she resisted. The question is, how does a teacher effectively respond? This chapter attempts to answer that question.

The Interviews: Colorblindess and More Emerge

All students in my first-year writing class that fall were invited, not required, to participate in the interview portion of this research project. Given her resistance already demonstrated in her writing and class responses, I was surprised but pleased and curious that Elaine volunteered. Like Annabell's and Roberta's, the first interview was immediately after their course, the second four years later, when they were seniors. I focused on this course as the impetus because of the kind of thinking, discussion and writing that the semester-long racism topic provoked, as previously described.

As Elaine spoke, I sat in horror, not wanting to close my office door for fear the venom would only get worse in a situation she might have perceived as even more safe to speak in racist ways, as happens in "backstage" homogenous racial groups (Houts Picca and Feagin). I had hoped, in the course of three and half more years of college since her first-year interview, she would have modulated her views, nurtured by other mind-opening courses and learning experiences. I had hoped that her first-year resistance was simply a stage. But listening to her in her senior interview, I felt alarm, confusion, and despair. I was afraid of her, of what I might have done in the class to cause this racist response, and whether or not I could ever respond adequately to so much hate and fear.

The odd thing was, Elaine was invariably smiling, very social, always reaching out to classmates to make some kind of connection. When a difference of some sort arose, there was always the quick shrug and another smile with a friendly but dismissive comment meant to show broad tolerance, such as, "To each his own!" or "Isn't that great?" Her mother, who died when Elaine was a young teen, had provided much everyday wisdom that Elaine often invoked. At one point in the interview, she told how she interpreted her mother's teaching in forming her own racial attitudes:

> Before [the class] I'd just ignore it [race] because I thought it was stupid. Because I was brought up, like I said before – my mother would tell me, you know, "Whites can do the same thing as Blacks, and it doesn't matter what their color is, they all can do the same things to you … Just don't be scared of someone because of their skin or their color or their -- their facial features and stuff like that. Everyone can act the same …"

From these words, it seems that Elaine's mother was probably trying to convey that people should be color-blind. As described by teacher education researchers Anita Tijerina Revilla, Amy Stuart Wells, and Jennifer Jellison Holme, color blindness is a White, privileged "argument that 'we are all the same' and that 'race does not matter'… as a way to avoid racial conflict and blatant racism …" (284). Rather than a marker of greater tolerance and racial understanding, color blindness is actually part of "the rhetoric of whiteness," according to sociologist, preacher and media star Michael Eric Dyson. In that rhetoric, he puts "equal playing field," "equal opportunity," and "reverse discrimination" as language intended to justify racist policy under the guise of fairness without regard to color (qtd. in Carlson 304). The effect then is that rather than deny that race exists, White color blindness denies that *racism* really happens.

Whether or not Elaine accurately reported what her mother actually said, Elaine interprets the message with an overlay of fear of difference. Instead of a sense of equality, her choice of words to describe her mother's racially color-blind stance conveys a victim stance for the (White) recipient because people, whether Black or White, "can all do the same things to you." In a strange color-blind twist, if everyone can act the same and Black people are dangerous, there is actually cause to fear everyone. In an interracial encounter, she does not see the potential for hands of equals joined in some shared endeavor, or even in a neutral position, but hands raised against her in racist threat.

Elaine may also have responded to what she *thought* was her mother's negative attitude about "outgroups," a phenomenon other researchers have found in studying the influence of parents' racial attitudes on adolescents (Helms "Beginnings" 94–97). So why does Elaine opt for a fearful interpretation? Some may write off her response as somewhat paranoid, something the average teacher would tiptoe around, not to irritate the animal. But rather than take an exceptional view of Elaine's response, it seems more useful to the instructor who faces many kinds of fear in her students to consider the specific racial dynamics operating in this fear that might be fruitfully addressed in a classroom setting.

Like the experience of many White people since the early days of this nation, Elaine's racial information has been shaped by institutions—schools, church, government, media—that were "racially hierarchical, white supremacist, and undemocratic. For the most part, they remain so today" (Feagin 5). For White students, college is often their first encounter with people and environments that include diversity of race, background, social class, sexual orientation, or beliefs, as mentioned earlier. As described in Chapter 2, Helms was among the first psychologists to popularize an understanding of racial identity development by naming separate stages of experience for Black and White people. Although now seen as more cyclical than linear, her stages for White students in the development of a positive White identity are: (1) contact, (2) disintegration, (3) re-integration, (4) pseudo-independence (5) immersion/emersion, (5), and autonomy ("Toward" 49–66). Elaine appears to be in the "contact" stage of racial identity development, which, in Helms's schema, occurs when Whites first realize "the actuality of Black people," ("Toward" 55) that is when they have some direct experience with actual Black people, not just hear about them from others. This stage is marked by "fearfulness and caution" and use of stereotypes in which "the White person uses the Black person to teach him or her about what Black people in general are like and often uses societal stereotypes of Blacks as the standard against which the Black person is evaluated" ("Toward" 57).

In Elaine's case, the class discussion of stereotypes and other topics about race forced her across a White boundary she hadn't known she needed to learn to cross. The more experienced students recognized racial stereotypes as, at least, socially unacceptable and could follow their critique in a video we used in class, *Race: The Power of an Illusion* (Adelman). However, Elaine struggled with the cognitive dissonance of having her beliefs labeled as stereotypes, perhaps for the first time. In her first interview with me, she said,

> And when we started talking about stereotypes I'd see someone of a particular race and think of their stereotype and like, "Oh, great, now I'm racist."… Well, I never really thought about it before, and then, when we started to talk about it in class, I'd see someone of a particular race and go, "Hmm, you know I wonder if they're on welfare cause I know most of their race is," or, "Hey, I bet he's got a gun." (*Laughs.*) You know, just how you're thinking that way. Well, after the stereotype – after you talk about -- you get to realize that kind of person is associated with this, and then you see them, and you go, "Hmm, I wonder, is that person the same way?" Or an African American'll get on the bus, a big brother man, and after we talked about, you know, how the stereotype is, I think, "Oh no." And then, I go, "Wait, what am I thinking about? Why has this changed me in this way before …"

What? I thought. Was she saying that our naming stereotypes made her believe in them? Did she really believe that? I wanted to shake that off; perhaps I misunderstood. After all, she also talked about how the course opened her, taught her more "just kind of about things—I guess—to open to a greater point of view." But in the next breath, she pulled away, as if her hand was too close to a flame: "And in a way, you almost wish you didn't want to know, cause then you wouldn't have to think about it with the stereotypes, you know," even as she reminded me repeatedly that her mother raised her to "not be scared of someone because of their skin color."

Clearly her comments and choice of words said she was scared, in spite of her mother's admonition. Right after telling about the frightening "big brother man" on the bus, she ranted about how quickly people can 'seem' racist to someone: "Just because, of the – you know, like I said, with the race game earlier, people get sued just for saying something when they might have not have meant it in a certain way, or not. It angers me that people can flip out so easy over something so simple …" She seemed to believe that the Others cause her fear as a kind of deliberate manipulation of her on their part, "the race game," making her aware of their race and, by extension, her fear of them. In Elaine's view, when she or other White people say something they may or may not intend as racial, they risk being sued by overly sensitive people of color. This reversal of responsibility for the fear she felt when she was made aware of someone's race (simply by their difference from her) is emblematic of "anxiety or arousal [that] may be present when actual interactions with Blacks are experienced or anticipated" by Whites in the earlier mentioned "contact" stage, according to Helms ("Toward" 57).

Anger about this fear seems to be the basis of White resistance to what's popularly called "reverse discrimination" and "political correctness." In explaining the relationship between fear and anger about it, rhetorician Marlia Banning identifies resentment as an aspect of White resistance to anti-racist argument that is cultivated by the powerful in our society to redirect the anger at injustice "laterally" (80), that is, against those at the same level rather than, more effectively and appropriately, against those who construct and maintain the power differentials that actually disadvantage those "lower" in the hierarchy. So, "the culture politic of resentment" is intended "to displace attention from a host of material changes in the U.S. that are eroding the social contract," such as the widening income gap, loss of real earning power and good-paying manufacturing jobs, the distortion of electoral voice by money politics, among other offenses. Banning argues that much of this resentment is played out on the racial stage: "A pivotal way in which this politic has been repeatedly deployed in public discourse appears under the umbrella of identity politics" (81). Although identity politics is not just race but also class, gender, sexual orientation, religion, and other identity markers, this dynamic certainly plays out in race-themed composition classes, such as the one in which Elaine and I worked together.

Banning explains that the just accusations and anger of most of the population who are not among the top-tier financially are displaced and redirected among themselves, deflected from their actual targets: the more powerful. In our course, the angers and resentment against Others surfaced in the discussion about "talk-radio" verbiage on reverse discrimination, welfare, Black-on-Black crime, children having children, absentee fathers, declining morals, hip-hop, disintegration of the family, the crack epidemic, and more. Banning argues that challenges to this dynamic are deemed inappropriate and not proper topics for discussion. Color-blindness actually feeds directly into this mechanism as it admonishes anyone who would challenge identity politics as racist. Thus, those who might rightly complain about their losses are silenced and their resentment smolders, as students like Elaine demonstrate.

Fear of Revealing Racism

Considering her unawareness of the prejudice inherent in her remarks, I was surprised when, at other times, Elaine spoke of imagining herself in the position of the two African American students in the class, one in each of the two first-year writing course sections studied. She worried that the African Americans might be offended, surprisingly not by the prejudice displayed by their classmates, but by the discussion of race itself. She felt it safer to talk about race in homogenous groups for fear of what she might unwittingly reveal, that she might "get scared of being around that person [of color] because they'll think I'm being racist." Her response recalls the social fears expressed by students that Trainor (*Rethinking Racism*) interviewed in a suburban high school class that was discussing racially-themed literature: they often don't fear *being* racist (because they know they are good people and good people aren't racist); they fear being mistaken for racist because they find it hard to express their rejection of negative emotions about life and people in ways that don't resort to lateral violence, that is the displaced resentment that Banning describes.

Trainor maintains that it is the "hidden curriculum" in high schools of positive thinking, individualism, and fairness confine student fear and other emotion to a narrow range of acceptable responses. She argues that school (and society at large) do not encourage students to examine openly the dissonance between lived experience of racism or classism and the curriculum intended to manage/control for appropriate feelings ("Teaching"). Like Trainor's students, Elaine felt the need to be cautious in how she spoke about race, particularly around students of color, and was very frank in her description of her difficulty in keeping her thoughts from slipping into racism against her will.

For example, Elaine noticed (or admitted for the first time that she noticed) a man's dark skin as she rode on the bus with him, which, she said, made her afraid that she would be falsely accused of stereotyping him. Later in the interview, though, her fear was more elemental: "I'm actually scared of the person for their stereotypical thing," that is that the person really was more prone to criminality, and that, as a result of becoming more aware of stereotypes, "now I think all these races are going to hurt me or—you know, just things like that, and I never thought that way before, and it makes me angry." She did have some awareness of her own complicity in this thought process because she said shortly after that, "But now from the class I think about people that way, and I'm mad at myself for it." To her credit, she was trying to reconstruct her White identity without its racist tendencies, but her repeated slides into illogical error and self-contradiction seem to reinforce her resistance to the racial critique, and she talked herself out of change. Unable to make sense of the continued existence of racism and her own participation in it, Elaine felt she could only deny it. She could not imagine a present anti-racist identity for herself that forgave her for her past, so she had to stay the same.

Some contend that an individual (or student) cannot work to develop a positive White identity, one that places her "beyond the role of victimizer" (Tatum 108) unless she first recognizes her Whiteness and the privilege that this society conveys on that color. If she could take responsibility for the privilege she enjoys, unconsciously or not, she could distance herself from the historical injuries of slavery, Jim Crow, Native American genocide, and other outcomes of racism. Without that awareness and acknowledgment, she is trapped in the role of victimizer, which is understandably unpleasant and uncomfortable. As mentioned before, Elaine was brought up not to "see" race and found the topic of the course tiresome, as reflected in her sympathy for her friend's 'fatigue':

> My friend at Penn State, he gets tired of it too because they – they talked about – um – uh – Asians a lot. And now every time he sees an Asian, and them talking in a different language he gets all ticked off and moves away from whoever it [inaudible]. Simply because he's tired of the racial – you know – bull – that's how he calls it. (*Laughs.*) …

Elaine also admitted her own disillusionment, "I got tired of the race stuff, but then I got used to it." Ratcliffe identifies this attitude of fatigue with the topic and unwillingness to challenge the current thinking as "dismissal," and "indifferent compliance," forms of resistance (138).

Eventually in the interviews, Elaine's resistance became angry, not at me but at the necessity to deal with racism, which she laterally displaced, as Banning says, on those who created the necessity: people of color. At one point, forgetting her own essays that she passionately wrote on injustice against Native Americans, Elaine launched into a diatribe against immigrants, along with African Americans (my question in italics):

> And then, a lot of people that I know get upset that certain racial identities get more privileges than – than American Whites do when we're the ones who live here – and things like that. *Against immigrants?* Yeah, immigrants, and … stuff like that. And then people who play – who play the racial game, you know? … [P]eople who don't choose to go on with their life or do more with it just because of their race or color. Like how we did the African American, um, thing, where there's more who are on welfare, more who don't have whole families and stuff like that. And a lot of people blame that's because of their race, when it's not, it's their own decision. And then it turns into an equal opportunity [inaudible] playing the race game. And then someone

> could say something, and then all of a sudden someone's freaking mad at you, telling you you're racist, and you weren't doing anything of that sort.

Elaine was clearly angry and resentful of others who threaten her privilege as a White person and resisted acknowledgment of others' rights and her own complicity in denying them their rights. Although I earlier identified Elaine as being in the "contact stage" of racial identity development, the kind of resistance displayed in the above quote is a White supremacist stance, a marker of another stage that Helms describes, the "reintegration stage," in which

> … the person consciously acknowledges a White identity. In the absence of contradictory experiences, to be White in America is to believe that one is superior to people of color. Consequently the Reintegration person accepts the belief in White racial superiority and Black inferiority. He or she comes to believe that institutional and cultural racism are the White person's due because he or she has earned such privileges and preferences. Race-related negative conditions are assumed to result from Black people's inferior social, moral, and intellectual qualities, and thus, it is not unusual to find persons in the Reintegration stage selectively attending to and/or reinterpreting information to conform to societal stereotypes of Black people ("Toward" 60).

Elaine's skewed interpretation of her mother's admonition to accept others regardless of their color and her active resistance to critical examination of racially stereotypical beliefs evidence the emotional and intellectual struggle provoked in her by the class experience. But the particulars of Elaine's journey belie a simple dismissal of her and other students like her as confirmed, irredeemable racists. She *wanted* to be liked—by *everyone*, including people who are purple, green, or whatever color, as she was so fond of describing her openness to others. And whether it was a desire to please and be pleasing to others that kept her engaged with me and the class, in spite of its threats to her identity, or something else, she worked hard to understand the course and its content, even as she resisted it.

New Learning and Resistance to It

Though constrained by her previous (in)experience, Elaine was aware that the race-themed college composition class invited some new thinking and skills development. In the first interview, Elaine took pains to assure me that she had learned things about writing and was proud of her new ability to consider a hot-button topic beyond a surface reaction:

> That was basically -- it was just delving deeper. You think of one thing, and then you have to – like you want to go on this – on this big, general basis, and then you have to break it down and go into smaller parts because race is a huge issue, and – you have to think about what you really want to get across, and sometimes that's quite difficult … Because it's such a huge topic … And because it's hotly debated ….

But awareness is not acceptance. Elaine didn't see the point of doing any border crossing. She felt that talking about race is only important to members of minority groups, and has no particular interest to White people:

> Maybe someone of a minority might think – might be grateful of it for the other people in the classroom -- to show them, you know, what kind of problems their racial identity has. But for me in particular, or for other classmates – you know, most people in our class um, I don't know if it would have – if it affected us in that kind of way, I guess. But I could see if you're, you know, Asian, or African American, and stuff, and you feel deeply about that, that yes, you would likely – you would likely just affect it, and show the other people in the class who weren't minorities.

To Elaine, the class was about demonstrating the difficulties of being non-White, but, in resistance, she makes a rhetorical move and dismisses race as topic relevant to a White person. Other White students, like Annabell, Roberta, and Madeline, who were less resistant to seeing and talking about race found ways to use compassion, a desire for intercultural competence, or a sense of responsibility for social justice as inroads to talking about race. But Elaine could not.

She also found comfort in the small size of the class (18) and, like Annabell and Roberta, the de facto segregation, again naming the fear of being seen as a racist:

> It would have been harder to talk about it that well … simply because you do not want to be seen as racist – at least I know I don't. And if you talk about – like when you start talking about the stereotypes and stuff, like I said, with some people who play the race game, or just get upset about stuff concerning their race, someone might have flipped out there in class, and no one would want to – might have not have wanted to say anything again in front of everybody … And I guess that goes with the whole, you know, new group with people of your own race, but it's merely just cause you're scared of what the other race is going to do if you say something wrong that might offend them.

While Elaine's concern for her classmate of color was laudable and showed some awareness of others' positions, she failed to see the causal link between White privilege and the learned awkwardness in discussions about race. She also blamed others for her fear of them and her discomfort at their oppressed status, not seeing her own complicity in reproducing such oppression. She liked an all-White group to avoid guilt, embarrassment, and possible challenge. Again, she was in a different place than the other students in relation to the class and the subject of race, which makes it all the more curious and perhaps hopeful that she volunteered for this study at all. The fact is, she did volunteer, even as she resisted, and as such, she is a living, breathing embodiment of the complexity of student learning and the real challenges of, to use Helen Fox's phrase, "unteaching racism" (Fox 5).

Teaching and Research Implications—My Doubts and Questions

The interview with Elaine raises many pedagogical and research concerns for me. Her interviews haunt me because they embody my insecurities about teaching critical pedagogy, about the accusation that I am bringing my personal ideology inappropriately into the classroom (Hairston). But I also believe, as feminist standpoint scholar Hallstein and others claim, that all teachers bring politics into the classroom by virtue of their own standpoint. For example, another feminist professor Susan Hekman quotes and summarizes French philosopher Foucault in saying, "… all visions are 'partial and perverse' in the sense that all knowledge is necessarily from some perspective; we must speak from somewhere and that somewhere is constitutive of our knowledge" (Hekman 345). In other words, cultural politics is inherent in all class content, particularly writing. Famed compositionists Berlin and Vivion quipped eloquently: "[D]iscursive practices are never the mere reflection of economic categories; they are always negotiated in power and politics, and power and politics are always negotiated in discursive practices" (ix). Thus Elaine could not help but respond in some way when the issue arose in her writing class because she brought with her all her own political, racial baggage to the task.

Despite Elaine's pain and struggle, at no time did she appear to bear any animosity towards me for having structured the class in a way that was obviously very distressing to her. It is this loyalty or perseverance or even perhaps courage that compels me to think and rethink the effects of and best practices in anti-racist pedagogy. I owe that to her and to all the students like her who come through my door. At the same time, I question my own reasons for continuing to employ anti-racist pedagogy. What if it doesn't make a difference or worse, does more harm than good with students like Elaine or others in the course who watch her, listen to her and witness my sometimes inadequate response to her? What does it say to the African American students that I tried to encourage her to say the taboos aloud so that we could examine them, knowing that she might still not "get" it and say even more racist things?

And what did that say to the White students who were embarrassed and disgusted by her words, wanting to distance themselves from her, dissatisfied with my tolerance of her confused and fearful discussion? Or worse, wondering if maybe she was right because I let her say it in the classroom and it resonated with their previous beliefs? As mentioned before, I found it incredibly difficult to record Elaine's interview responses without protest. I sometimes found my role as teacher/interviewer/observer to be in direct conflict with my instincts and impulses as an instructor committed to anti-racism. It is very hard not to respond negatively to students' muddled thinking and racist comments. Sometimes, my dismay at the depths of the prejudice Elaine and other students have revealed has somewhat incapacitated me: I become angry at what appears to be their ignorance and obstinacy. How dare they treat other human beings with such disregard? My empathy goes out the window, and I become unable to imagine what in their experience or worldview might prompt such hatred, cloaked in trite aphorisms, hearsay, and regurgitation of right-wing talk-radio.

I also become defensive of my course, the decisions I've made in structuring it, and of anti-racist pedagogy in general. How dare they treat *me* that way? Such challenge to my authority as teacher seems bold and rude, at least. Their resistance becomes a personal rejection of me as a person, perhaps even me as a White person. The conventions of classroom decorum fall away in those moments and we are strangers staring across a gulf: I don't know them and they don't know me.

There have also been times when I've had to look in the mirror and question my own motives. For example, during the latest interview with Elaine, I was half aware but unwilling to take action to protect a dear friend and colleague, an African American woman who, working as the administrative assistant just outside my office door, was an unwitting, unwilling, silent witness to the interview. Her situation bore uncomfortable similarity to that of students of color in my classes, trapped and voiceless in a racist space. My colleague later rightly questioned my role in that incident, objecting to my silence in the face of Elaine's cutting remarks. What was my purpose? Why didn't I confront Elaine's racism? How was that teaching?

So, if a teacher believes the politics are already in the classroom and is committed to using cultural studies, critical race theory, and/or critical pedagogy to help students learn to negotiate appropriate, perhaps liberating discursive practices, how does she respond to the resistance of students like Elaine, especially when it spills out into hurtful language against the teacher, other students, or innocent bystanders? Are there ways to have more choices than either to suffer the pain and awkwardness of these moments or to silence the offender? And was my defense to my African American friend genuine, that I was doing research and couldn't stop or correct what Elaine was saying without distorting the interview results? Or was it some kind of cowardice that left me speechless and passive before Elaine's rant?

I also wonder a lot about student voice: are students wrong until they agree with me? Don't I have an obligation to show them the flaws in their logic and the errors in their facts? But the lesson they sometimes reveal they have learned in comments on student evaluations is that there is one right way to think and that they should just be quiet until the class is over and they can escape safely with their grade (and beliefs) intact. How do we persuade and engage them in new ideas without silencing them? Do I have the strength to back down and recognize that we may have to agree to disagree, at least for now or am I chickening out, failing to hold them and myself accountable?

It's obvious that I don't have this difficulty sorted out. I derive hope from those in the field who have begun to define some avenues of theory and research that begin to address the root causes and compassionate, intelligent response to student (and teacher) fear. They seem to be saying that, given understanding of the sources and dynamics of this fear, teachers can and should continue to press against the resistance they encounter from fearful students. They point to the hope and belief that teachers can formulate strategies that will (1) assure fearful students that their experience is understood, (2) help fearful students perceive alternate interpretations of their experience and/or remain open to hearing others' different experiences, and (3) allay the teachers' own defensive responses to students acting out of fear.

It is too easy to say there are no easy answers and move on. Real people like Elaine and real teachers need feasible, effective strategies that may not end racism but will help them engage in this struggle together, responsibly, with compassion and fairness to everyone concerned. Teachers need to find more ways to do this work and they need to bring the concerns of all parties into this mix, not simply those who are most receptive.

What I Wish I Had Said

One of the most powerful of questions to ask someone caught in a difficult race moment is really two related questions that I wish I had asked Elaine more: What is your story? Where did this reaction come from? Until people believe they are heard and understood, they feel compelled to tell their own story even in the face of others' pain or contravening evidence. Despite what teachers believe, facts generally do not change minds. Instead human beings give primacy to their strong, emotionally-inflected version of the truth and show active fear, as previously discussed about Elaine, when their view of the world is threatened.

As mentioned earlier, Trainor has theorized "emotioned beliefs" and argues that the "persuasive appeal of racist discourses is affective and emotioned, rather than logical or rational, and that it is rooted not in abstract political or identity-based calculations but in local experiences and feelings that are given force in school" (*Rethinking Racism* 3). In her research, she paid attention to the "emotioned rules" that were "implicit norms of behavior, attitude, intellectual habits, values, and practices that were taught and enforced via emotional exhortations in school" (Trainor *Rethinking Racism* 23). Thus, presentations of facts and other objective evidence that logically argue the persistence of racism or White people's role in racism cannot compete with the deeply rooted beliefs in the value of hard work (vs. lazy poverty) or the need to maintain a positive attitude (vs. a critical one), for example, that have become embedded in and wed to racist discourses. Using the question, "Where does that come from?" invites students to return to the site of that emotioned belief, recognize it, and re-examine how it pulls them in (racist) directions they may not be aware of nor desire.

The question creates an opportunity for students to apply a new tool to an old emotioned lesson. Tatum notes that "When people don't have the tools for moving forward, they tend to return to what is familiar, often becoming more vigorous in their defense of the racial status quo than they were initially" (Tatum 105). An extreme example of that can be found in certain types of sexual violence prevention programming. In some cases, when gender roles, particularly male dominance and aggression are not directly addressed in sexual violence prevention programming, student attitudes "revert to previous levels within months, men's rape-supportive attitudes sometimes increase" (Burn 780). Extended to anti-racist programming, students who are not permitted the opportunity to directly address their emotional attachment to aspects of their racist past, in spite of their guilt about it, may reject and even become more pronounced in their racist stances.

The question "Where did that story come from?" helps the student speaker, as well as all the classroom witnesses, begin to understand the source of a particular racist discourse and develop some empathy for the speaker, whether or not they agree with her. Such empathy is a stronger motivator than guilt (Iyer 355) and lays the foundation for productive dialogue that simultaneously recognizes the privilege of the dominant racial group while creating a pathway for inclusive, responsible problem solving to create social change (Zuniga et al. 15).

While I did ultimately encourage Elaine to keep looking for answers and to ask her one African American friend to tell her more about her own experience, I tried to assure Elaine that I understood that she was afraid. Not that I understood or agreed with her misplaced fear, but that I had heard how new and hard this experience was for her. As one faculty member described it in a workshop on racial dialogue with me, the role of the teacher is to convey with nods, perhaps, or other body language, that she is listening without judgment, encouraging the person's speaking without approving the sentiment or beliefs conveyed in the words.

As for the students who are unwilling subjects/witnesses/victims of another student's fear-laden story, we must care for them as well. I did apologize to my friend, the administrative assistant outside my office door where I interviewed, for having overheard Elaine's story. I tried to humbly acknowledge her pain and the history of pain caused by White people. I'm sure that was insufficient but I haven't found a better approach than honesty about my inadequacy. In Chapter 6, I will discuss more about the dynamics of working with students of color.

The work of race talk is undeniably difficult, seeming to have no good entry or, at times, clear, ethical exit. But teachers' willingness to intervene, calming their own fears as well as those of the student, trying to recognize and name the fear, other emotion, and misinformation at the root of the reaction, until perhaps the practice becomes more a more manageable, habitual response to the many kinds of new learning inherent in race talk wherever and whenever it needs to happen.

For Elaine, there were many things that might have provided her a safe port. A teacher is only one person, but if she has done enough of her own homework in racial identity development, and has found some support in the faculty and the institution, she will not feel totally blind-sided by the fearful displaced reactions of students—or other faculty—like Elaine. Teachers can learn to overcome their own fear of appearing racist, and how to teach students how to use familiar rhetorical tools to examine false racial logic and false equivalencies between the positivism of good citizenship and damaging, ultimately divisive color blindness. Teachers who employ compassionate listening paired with critical challenges to habitual prejudice can provide pathways out of the racial morass for students like Elaine, reducing the collateral damage to other students, especially students of color, like Madeline. As the next chapter reveals, the missed opportunity to create such change lived right there in that classroom, right between Elaine and Madeline, as well as many others. If only I had known then what I know now, we all might have learned something different.

Works Cited

Adelman, Larry. *Race: The Power of an Illusion*. Film, California Newsreel Independent Television Service, 2003.

Banning, Marlia E. "The Politics of Resentment." *JAC*, vol. 26, no. 1–2, 2006, pp. 65–101.

Berlin, James and Michael Vivion. "Introduction: A Provisional Definition." *Cultural Studies in the English Classroom*, edited by James Berlin and Michael Vivion. Boynton/Cook, 1992, pp. vii–xiv.

Burn, Shawn Meghan. "A Situational Model of Sexual Assault Prevention through Bystander Intervention." *Sex Roles*, vol. 60, 2009, pp. 779–792.

Carlson, Dennis. "Narrating the Multicultural Nation: Rosa Parks and the White Mythology of the Civil Rights Movement." *Off-White: Readings on Power, Privilege, and Resistance*, edited by Michelle Fine et al. Routledge, 2004, pp. 302–311.

Feagin, Joe R. *Racist America: Roots, Current Realities, and Future Reparations*. Routledge, 2000.

Fox, Helen. *"When Race Breaks Out": Conversations About Race and Racism in College Classrooms*. vol. 6. Peter Lang, 2004. *Questions About the Purpose(S) of Colleges & Universities*, Norm Denizen, Josef Progler, Joe L. Kincheloe, Shirley R. Steinberg.

Hairston, Maxine. "Diversity, Ideology, and Teaching Writing." *Cross-Talk in Comp Theory: A Reader*, edited by Victor Villanueva, 2nd edition. NCTE, 1992, pp. 697–713.

Hallstein, D. and O'Brien Lynn. "Where Standpoint Stands Now: An Introduction and Commentary." *Women's Studies in Communication*, vol. 23, no. 1, 2000, pp. 1–15, Thomson Gale Expanded Academic ASAP.

Hekman, Susan. "Truth and Method: Feminist Standpoint Theory Revisited." *Signs: Journal of Women in Culture & Society*, vol. 22, no. 2, 1997, p. 341+, Academic Search Elite.

Helms, Janet E. "The Beginnings of a Diagnostic Model of Racial Identity." *Black and White Racial Identity: Theory, Research, and Practice*, edited by Janet E. Helms. Praeger, 1993, pp. 83–104.

—. "Toward a Model of White Racial Identity Development." *Black and White Racial Identity: Theory, Research, and Practice*, edited by Janet E. Helms. Praeger 1993, pp. 49–66.

Houts Picca, Leslie and Joe R. Feagin. *Two-Faced Racism: Whites in the Backstage and the Frontstage*. Routledge, 2007.

Iyer, Aarti, Colin Wayne Leach, and Anne Pedersen. "Racial Wrongs and Restitutions: The Role of Guilt and Other Group-Based Emotions." *Off-White: Readings on Race, Privilege, and Resistance*, edited by Lois Weis, Michelle Fine, Linda Powell Pruitt, April Burns, 2nd edition. Routledge, 2004, pp. 345–361.

Ratcliffe, Krista. "Rhetorical Listening: A Trope for Interpretive Invention and a 'Code of Cross-Cultural Conduct'." *College Composition and Communication*, vol. 51, no. 2, 1999, pp. 195–224.

Revilla, Anita Tijerina et al. ""We Didn't See Color": The Salience of Color Blindness in Desegregated Schools." *Off-White: Readings on Power, Privilege and Resistance*, edited by Michelle Fine et al., Second edition. Routledge, 2004, pp. 284–301.

Tatum, Beverly Daniel. "*Why Are All the Black Kids Sitting Together in the Cafeteria?*" *And Other Conversations About Race*. Basic Books, 2003.

Trainor, Jennifer Seibel. *Rethinking Racism: Emotion, Persuasion, and Literacy Education in an All-White High School*. Southern Illinois University Press, 2008.

—. *Teaching to Transgress?: (Re)Constructing Race, Class and Gender in School*. Course syllabus, University of Pittsburgh, 2002.

Zuniga, Ximena et al. "Intergroup Dialogue in Higher Education: Meaningful Learning About Social Justice." *Jossey-Bass Higher and Adult Education Series*, edited by Kelly Ward and Lisa E. Wolf-Wendel, vol. 32, no. 4. Report, Association for the Study of Higher Education, Winter 2007.

· 6 ·

MADELINE

Madeline could talk an arm off the Venus de Milo. A student who identified as Middle Eastern but appeared White, due to her Irish heritage, she loved the opportunity to "finally" talk about race, racism, and White privilege in America, particularly in our city and our university. Her experience had been, as women's studies professor Patti Duncan describes, full of racist insults of students of color, including "invisibility, erasure, stereotyping, violence, economic disenfranchisement, and other forms of racism and oppression" (45). Madeline heard peers reject with disbelief and repugnance what she experienced and passionately believed. Teachers mocked her political stances as naive and biased toward people of color and limited her time to talk in class. It seemed everyone at school and in Pittsburgh lived in a different world that didn't see or "get" what she thought was obvious, common sense; she was out of place, out of sync, and alone, and no one would listen to her protest about this situation. She found herself, as Duncan describes, generally "misrepresented or completely excluded from the curriculum," with "few people like themselves … [as] role models, mentors, and even friends with whom to share common experiences, often resulting in a profound sense of isolation" (45). As a result, she loved the platform our class on racism and writing provided and was nearly giddy to talk to me about it.

As the only student of color in this project and one of few in the class itself, Madeline's stories and opinions provide insights on the student who brings to the classroom an experience of difference unlike most of her White classmates, causing her to struggle to find her footing, her voice, and her identity. But she was finding it. Like other students of color, she had thought about her racial identity far more than her White classmates had (Tatum 53–54). Notably, although she strongly identified as Middle Eastern, she was also very aware of her White appearance and the privilege that conveyed. Employing a complex, nuanced understanding of her own combined target and agent identities (Harro 17), she actively resisted the White cultural norm in the class and did not hesitate to point out the flaws of and gaps in her classmates' analysis of the intersections between racism and the social problems they were researching. Among her peers that I interviewed, she had the most fully integrated understanding of both the personal and institutional features of racism, grounding her belief in the necessity of political action for social justice.

Predictably enough, her narrative challenged her classmates, myself, her instructor, and the university: how can a critical classroom pedagogy meet the divergent, even oppositional needs of the students of color who are already keenly aware of the failure of our society to adequately grapple with and resolve racial inequity? At the same time, how can the classroom educate and hold accountable the White students, their White teachers and institutions, who fearfully and sometimes defiantly resist awareness of racism's persistence and their complicity in maintaining a "white racial frame" (Feagin)? These are the questions I wish to address in this chapter by examining Madeline's interviews.

Recognizing "Weirdness" and Other Differences

Together Madeline's two interviews lasted over two hours while her classmates' interviews lasted from 30 to 75 minutes. Madeline's volubility may have come from several sources. Like her peers, she was very conscious of my role as her teacher, an authority figure, giving me an inordinate amount of credit in her first-year interview for having significantly changed her because she decided it was sexist to use "man" as if it were a gender-neutral word. So her willingness, even eagerness, to talk to me could have been an effort to please the person in charge. This kind of reinforcement from an authority figure may have been particularly important to her because she did not identify with most of her peers and had difficulty with some of her other instructors.

Her desire to talk longer than her peers may also have been part of her effort to process her mixed racial identity. As she said, she didn't get much chance to talk to people about race issues that she was facing. Although ethnically Lebanese, Madeline looked like a "little White girl," as she described herself, and often felt negatively stereotyped by her White skin. She seemed eager to assure her listeners that she was not just another privileged White person who didn't "get" people of color.

In spite of her appearance, or perhaps because of it, she wanted to be recognized as not White:

> I identify as a Middle Eastern person. I am very open about that. If a conversation about terrorism or something comes up, I say I am Middle Eastern and my grandmother, one generation behind me, is 100% Middle Eastern. The only thing is looking at me or my sister, you cannot tell. It doesn't always bring a welcome response but our heritage is very important to us.

As her last sentence suggests, she felt it both a blessing and curse to be set apart from others: a blessing to be unrelated to a negative White identity, a curse to be seen as Other.

Understandably she did not like being associated with Arab stereotypes because "being Arab doesn't make you a terrorist." She felt singled out negatively:

> While in college, I was frequently asked what I was, because I never noticed until people started asking me but in the summer when it gets warm my hair gets curly people assume, Are you Cuban? Are you Italian? Are you Spanish? And I tell people I'm Middle Eastern and people start making terrorist jokes and ask how many people my people killed and really nasty, nasty things. I've been called a sand-jockey, a sand-n-word, a lot of nasty things. I never thought about it before but I think it's weird that you can look at me and say, You're not one of us! I thought it was really weird …

"Weird", I realized eventually, was Madeline's euphemism for "racist." As she said, she had never encountered this kind of ethnic and racial scrutiny before, which shocked her but also pleased her as a way to distinguish herself from her classmates whom she discovered were very "weird."

She found it hard to deal with her White classmates' racism, as unintentional as it often was. She tried to develop an empathic understanding of how their experiences must have misshapen their perspectives, but it was a struggle for her:

> I mostly remember White blond girls. That sounds really terrible. I don't remember my classes being very racially diverse. I think the attitudes were very diverse. I think some people were brought up to be very understanding or were brought up to not be so much. Some of each were brought up to be very quiet and some were brought up to very loud. It can be a good thing and a bad thing. But I noticed a lot of people who weren't open to mixed race or who didn't believe racism existed. They didn't see anything wrong in not believing that racism existed. I remember that being a prominent quality of people. I also remember that for being such a giving school where you were supposed to want to help people, there weren't a lot of people who were very motivated.

This comment came from her senior interview, some five years after the class, an indication of how alienated she felt in the first-year class, how deeply they had offended her.

Another encounter, also still vivid after five years, was about the student who sat next to her, whom ironically was Elaine, the student from the previous chapter. Although Madeline couldn't recall the specifics of the moment, the emotion was still very present and alive to her:

> I remember the girl who sat next to me. I don't remember her name but she was very White and had red hair and was very, very pro-White, and I thought it was really weird. I think the first time I discovered this was when I was writing my paper on rap … .and I remember everyone picking on me for it. Everyone was weird about it. But I remember her being very—I forget what it was, but it was something really odd though. It couldn't have been like White supremacy, but it was very close, and I remember just not knowing what to say to her. I cannot remember who she was but I remember she sat next to me, and her complaining, and I remember other girls complaining about "Why do we have to look at racism?" What do I say? "Just let me hang out with the KKK! If *you* like Black people, it's cool" (italics mine). I didn't know what to say, but I remember being shocked, real shocked.

As she talked, she continually looked to me for validation, seeming to hope that I would fill in the blanks in her story and understand her distress. Madeline clearly hesitated to name Elaine's "pro-White" attitudes as racist, not even wanting to call them "White supremacy" although they clearly were. But taken aback by such comments and attitudes, she fought to find sufficient common ground with her classmates to even begin to talk about their contrasting experiences of diversity.

Difference—and Racism—Experienced as Chasm

The gulf between her own experiential understanding of racism and that of her classmates lead to academic difficulties. Take as illustration her difficulty with the peer review of her classmates' essays, an essential and graded component of our class. Like many students as long-time writing program administrator Brian Huot points out, Madeline consistently confined herself in peer feedback to a focus on only grammar and mechanics errors (Huot 68). To move beyond that level, she may have needed better scaffolding in the curriculum or other institutional structures to directly address student skills in assessment of texts (Huot 67–68).

But Madeline did know more than she let on, held back not by rhetorical knowledge as much as her confusion about how to grapple with her classmates' subtle and not-so-subtle racism. Peer review created for her a kind of too-close encounter as she was caught between the desire to help and be part of the group and her shock at their implicit and even overt bias. The affront of her classmates' racism created a moral dilemma for Madeline. Her voice angry and incredulous, she related how she reached a breaking point, explaining that she felt obliged to object to their attitudes and to more substantial peer review, just to avoid complicity in their racism:

> There's a fine line between fixing grammar and fixing ethical problems in a paper. Your sentence is grammatically correct but … This paper is like, I can't help you. It's outside my moral code to tell you where to put commas and periods in your hater paper. I can't do that. I can't help you.

Obviously, this was more than beginning writer reticence. I believe Madeline did not feel safe enough with them to challenge their illogic or "weirdness."

In retrospect I realize now that Madeline and her classmates needed more support to be able to talk about their differences; in this highly racialized society in which talk about race is labeled racist, people often do not have the dialogue skills to even begin to address their separate realities. So not only was Madeline left with the delicate task of pointing out the illogic of an argument in a peer's paper, but she would have had to overcome her classmates' "strategic color blindness," as social psychologist Evan Apfelbaum and colleagues name it: "We propose that when placed in the ambiguous and often threatening context of race-relevant social interaction, one approach many Whites adopt is *strategic colorblindness*: avoidance of talking about race—or even acknowledging racial difference—in an effort to avoid the appearance of bias" (918). It would be (was) unfair to expect Madeline to confront all of that on her own in the context of a peer review. I should have made this issue visible in conversations with the entire class. Instead I regrettably put that burden on Madeline's shoulders alone, further isolating her and abandoning my responsibility for reasons that were as strategically color-blind as the students.'

Faced repeatedly with situations like this, it's no surprise that Madeline's alienation and isolation from the others in the class ran deep: "After that class, people didn't talk to me much. Students didn't talk to me. My only friends after my sophomore year were four African American moms who sometimes took day classes but normally took night classes. They were my only friends. So we would all talk." Judging from her frustration with other students, I'm sure their "talk" was much different from those of her White peers. Mostly, despite her volubility, she felt her racial difference was deliberately ignored and her voice was silenced. When I asked in her senior interview if she felt it was harder or easier for her to recognize and engage with racism because of the awareness raised in the first-year class, she noted how her own passionate advocacy was reined in by her environment:

> [Racism] was easier for me to look at and analyze but I think [it was] because of how much we delved into it and how passionate I got. Other people do not share that passion. There were racist people in my classes. There were racist people everywhere but I think because I was so comfortable with [talking about] it, that made it more difficult because there were people who did not share my sentiment so at times I would just stop talking. There are times when you know you just cannot talk.

Silenced by the social norms that denigrated her differences as a woman of color, Madeline gave up on people—the class, other classes, and White people in general—as a means to work out her own ideas about race, racism and identity.

Strategies for Resilience

Notably though, Madeline had developed and was developing an array of strategies that helped her live in her complex identity in a world that kept trying to pigeonhole her. In an example of complicated social resilience, she recalled her first-year habit of going out to clubs and parties that were perceived as non-White with friends of color as a kind of protection against the negative attitudes she might receive as an apparent, out-of-place White person: "There are places that my friends [of color] want to go that are mostly minority. I want to have friends with me because I don't want to appear to be the only little White girl there because I get picked on. It has happened." She felt more comfortable among people of color but was also aware that not everyone would be as comfortable with her and that she could face more unwelcome scrutiny of her skin color and motives. She felt that by recruiting allies of color, she could confront the challenges of people of color to her White skin in a Black space, telegraph her true identity and acceptance of people of color, and distance herself from the racism of some of her White classmates, like Elaine.

In a complicated twist, by going to the clubs with friends of color, she was also using her White skin privilege as a political move, a "racial literacy project" to "dismantle racial hierarchies" (Twine 407). Twine refers to racial literacy projects in her study of White parents who "rather than training their [multiracial] children to deploy their Whiteness in ways that distance them from other African-descent people, are teaching them to strongly identify with the political and cultural struggles of black people" (407). Making a similar move in a different context, Madeline allied her apparently White self with people of color in the dance club, a public place, to simultaneously send a message to White people that Black spaces (and people) are not tainted or inferior. She felt it important to overtly express the empathy she felt for people of color who continually faced racial microaggressions. In the following passage, she recalled how some of the class readings, like McIntosh's list of White privileges, helped her better recognize and understand how others' experiences of racial discrimination were both like and different from her own life as an apparently White person in a racialized society:

> I have become more aware of the limitations that are on people because of their race. I knew racism was a problem but I didn't understand what it was and is and I didn't understand the intensity of restrictions on people who are not White when you look at them. [The class] made me aware of how terrible it must be. Like going to [the] grocery store [is different]. I can avoid going to that club but [not] the grocery store. If you are the only person who looks like that, and that's how people judge people by what you look like. I've become much more aware of that since I was a freshman.

Madeline was deliberately cultivating increased racial literacy and empathy for other people of color, including those who misunderstood and stereotyped her as an unsympathetic, racist White person. By finding ways to club in locales most popular with people of color, she was satisfying her own need to be herself among people of color while also taking a public stand, what some have called being a White race traitor (George; Wise *Speaking* 4). By critically comparing her own privileged experience in grocery stores and other places and situations, she opened herself to a non-dominant perspective, effectively giving up her White privilege and increasing her agency.

But at other times she defended her own lack of privilege as someone others identified with terrorists, as earlier mentioned. She vehemently objected to rigid lines between races, not in a color-blind way but as a person with a multiracial identity who embodies resistance to racial categorization. I use "multiracial" in this chapter to refer to Madeline's heritage with apology. Terms like multiracial, biracial, multi-ethnic and others are unavoidably fraught with historical meaning, recalling imperialistic racial categorization (quadroon, octaroon, etc.) and racist belief in race as biological. To talk about "race" at all is to validate the paradigm, yet the way out of racism is to critically deconstruct and talk about it. For further discussion of this points, see Chapter 1 of *Racecraft: The Soul of Inequality in American Life* by sociologist Karen E. Fields and historian Barbara J. Fields.

Thus to deny Madeline personal freedom (privilege) to wear what she wanted, for example, was to deny her complex racial identity. She told a story of criticism she suffered from her peers, including Black "girls," for wearing Apple Bottoms t-shirts, a brand developed by Black rapper Nelly:

> They're really nice jeans, and the shirts are really nice, and it's for curvy girls. My sister and I both got a shirt. One of her friends walked up to her and was like, "Do you know you're wearing Black people clothes?" People say that to me too. I'm like, I didn't know you have such a problem with who can wear what name-brands!

There are several interesting layers in this story that speak to the complexity of Madeline's negotiation of her racial identity. Her sister's friends may have been reading her shirt as White appropriation of clothing culturally identified as belonging to African Americans, a disingenuous effort to associate herself with the cool rapper or the anti-fashion of hip-hop (The Center for Engaged Research and Collaborative Learning (CERCL) Writing Collective 48). Both non-White and White peers may have found this puzzling and/or offensive for all the reasons of disrespect and imperialism that racial or cultural appropriation is still very hotly contested space. Witness almost two decades of debates about White rapper Eminem's right to claim his art (Dawkins), the uproars over the revelations that Rachel Dolezal, the former president of the Spokane NAACP (formerly the National Association of Colored People) is

White (Johnson et al.; Wise "Mimicry"), and even the same for the formerly anonymous creators of the blog Thug Kitchen (Butler), among other displays.

It's hard to say that Madeline wasn't trying to appropriate "cool" but she may also have been trying to say something else. As Thompson and Haytko explain,

> ...[F]ashion discourses provide consumers with a plurality of interpretive positions that, because of their diverse associations, can enable them to juxtapose opposing values and beliefs. Consumers use these countervailing meanings of fashion discourse to address a series of tensions and paradoxes existing between their sense of individual agency (autonomy issues) and their sensitivity to sources of social prescription in their everyday lives (conformity issues). (15–16)

Madeline understood that her clothing was making a statement about her, although it is not clear exactly what that fashion identity statement was or, more importantly, whether it was an outright rejection of African Americans' exclusive claims to Nelly's fashion branding. She certainly understood racially encoded behavior but seemed to resist its complexity at times. In spite or perhaps because of her anti-racist commitment, she knew she crossed a line in her clothing choice of Apple Bottoms but wanted to be able to define the meaning of that action herself. She seemed to be saying that race doesn't matter, when she knew from her own experience that it does, and that only a White person in denial of the social realities of U.S. society would or could say that. As Peggy McIntosh has noted, White people have the privilege of not considering the impact of their actions; they see themselves (and society sees them) as individuals, whereas people of color are often read as representative of their group (qtd. in Tatum 8). As if she were color blind to her own White skin and to the African American cultural claims to the Nelly brand, Madeline declared the right to wear what she wanted, seeming to ignore how that might be read by White and Black people alike, glossing over the White privilege she was exerting by making a unilateral decision without regard for its possible offense of African Americans. Why? Was she expressing her anger at being excluded from minority status? Or was she again rejecting racial categorization, even if it offended the population with which she wanted to be allied?

The argument could be made that her clothing was also part of her racial literacy project, that as a hidden person of color, Madeline was enacting a reverse of what counseling psychologist Derald Wing Sue calls "impression management" in which she confronted the "politeness protocol" in racial dialogue (*Race* 61–64) and challenged a racially inflected clothing norm as part of her public statement of her identity. She was inviting a conversation about race, about *her* race. Her encounters with others, though, seem to say that this particular tactic was not exactly successful, further alienating her from a peer group of any color.

In Two Countries

Madeline's dual majority/minority sense of self in relation to others and against her own apparent social interests was very typical of much of her interviews and seems a key component of her multiracial ethnic identity. In a model of ethnic identity development developed by Jean Phinney, a developmental psychologist, Madeline seemed to be engaged in a second-stage "ethnic identity search, when individuals are actively engaged in defining for themselves what it means to be a member of their own racial or ethnic group" (qtd. in Tatum 132). Her multiracial identity allowed and called her to act as a visible bridge between racial countries, demonstrating the false borders between those artificially created countries, embodying the lie of racial categories and actively deconstructing the false social norms of "racecraft" that Fields and Fields explain, as mentioned earlier. The term "racecraft," coined by Karen E. Fields and Barbara J. Fields, "highlights the ability of pre- or non-scientific modes of thought to hijack the minds of the scientifically literate" (6), like witchcraft, to create an entire mythological world of categorization of racial difference and make it seem real.

Madeline's project was to embody and make clear that race is an illusion to which people have attached harmful significance to the detriment of all society. In effect, Madeline is traversing the territory from non-racist to anti-racist:

> Being *nonracist* means soul searching, individual change, and working on the self; becoming *antiracist* means taking personal action to end external racism that exists systemically and in the action of others ... Studies suggest that antiracist people have greater racial diversity among friends, support affirmative action, possess greater cultural sensitivity and empathy, and are more prone to take action to rectify injustices. (Sue *Race* 159, 162)

Alienated from others by her fuller racial identity understanding but increasingly comfortable in publicly battling for her identity, Madeline often danced back and forth across racial lines, and framed that agility as a source of her power to create social change. She recalled arguing repeatedly in her papers the importance of teaching young children to accept and understand difference positively, believing that early education would help children cope better with diversity as they grew up. In one story she told about her daycare center job, she described the pain of witnessing very young children struggle with their non-dominant racial identities:

> When I was working and when I was going to school people would ask me [about my racial identity] and lots of things. When I was working down at the daycare, the kids are like, "Miss [Madeline], I wasn't born the right color!" This isn't OK. My workout was that the little kids [would] notice and I'd have to tell them sometimes people are mean because I had to learn the hard way that people are mean. … If I say I am Middle Eastern and I'm proud of being Middle Eastern, it shouldn't change your opinion of me. It shouldn't matter what I am or what I look like, and it did, and I never thought it would. It really opened my eyes a lot because I never thought somebody would ask me what I was.

Frequently challenged on and denied her own racial identity, Madeline felt she deeply understood the children's experiences in the daycare center as part of that same rejection and alienation she herself had experienced. She truly hurt for them and felt moved to action.

Rather than succumb to the enormous and painful pervasiveness of racism and its being passed from generation to generation right before her eyes at the daycare, she framed the challenge as a racial literacy project in Twine's terms or her "workout" as she called it. She felt she should explain in age-appropriate terms that sometimes people are racist ("mean"), that it's unfair and wrong, that she too had experienced racism, and that they do have allies in people like herself. She modeled for those children the entire spectrum of racial identity development from encounter with one's difference through immersion in its pain, then internalization and development of an oppositional identity, to commitment to liberation (Tatum 55; Wise *Speaking* 357). Her project—her "workout"—was to stand by those children and provide a counter narrative to White supremacy for them to adopt and, hopefully, change the world. She professed repeatedly that the children were her hope, our hope, probably one that sustained her through the difficulties posed by her experience at a predominantly White college.

Madeline's response to the existence of racism in her life and in society was starkly different from two of her classmates who also participated in this study. When threatened with difference, Elaine professed palpable fear and retreated to stereotype to help her recognize danger and make sense of "good" and "bad" in the world. Roberta longed for social change but couldn't sustain much personal involvement in it. Madeline, on the other hand, professed she was "very interested in race, … liberal hippieish," and "a very emotional hippie person" which made her laugh at herself ruefully.

Justifying her belief and hope for change in teaching children how to deal with difference differently, she cited her own home experience as a crucible for her racial awareness and flexibility. Like many anti-racists (Sue *Race* 162), she had grown up with and maintained a diverse group of friends:

> My friends from home do involve people of color. I have a friend who is biracial, a friend from Pakistan, I have friends of all different colors and they are very good friends of mine. We share things about our backgrounds. I am Middle Eastern and that's always a big thing. We have parties and my friends from Pakistan are always a big hoot. They are always sharing things about Pakistan or talk about the different things. My biracial friend gets picked on all the time and so does my friend from Pakistan. You can tell by looking at them they are different and people call them racial slurs. They don't call <u>me</u> racial slurs so it's a lot more noticeable. We are close and it's a lot more open in my group of friends.

She continued to socialize on weekends when she could with this supportive group, even as she lived at college. Experientially, she knew what researchers have found, that "well intentioned Whites are disinclined to enforce egalitarian norms because of the cognitive and emotional toll required to do so," leaving the White ally to experience "invalidation and marginalization from significant others, which can be quite painful" (Sue *Race* 161). Madeline's group of friends knew how to negotiate minority status, including its downsides in a predominantly White society. They provided for her a peer group who would stand by her against social norms in which, as Sue again summarizes, "the chasm between awareness and [antiracist] action is quite large" (161).

This kind of support contrasts sharply with the lack of support other students in this study experienced for social justice action. Annabell found herself standing alone as the "joke-killer." Roberta was overwhelmed and silenced, without a sense of the possible ways to gain voice. And Elaine retreated entirely to safety among Whites like herself. Unlike the other students, Madeline was confident there were others "out there" like herself who knew how to live diversity and find solace in each other's support.

That's not to say that she didn't struggle with her mult-racial anti-racist identity. College often forced her out of her supportive diverse friend group, probably because she lived at school, away from them. Thus, in addition to the "weird" questions about her identity, she often found herself in an outsider's position, both as an apparent White person and as a Middle Easterner. For example, as other students talked about the presence of gender and racial slurs in popular songs, rap, and conversation, including the n-word, Madeline reacted strongly:

> When people talk badly about girls in songs, and people using the N-word, that really bothered me, and I started explaining it to people. So many people know not to use racial slurs around me. And girls will tell me, "Oh, my boyfriend uses that term, but, uh, he's not racist." You can't use the n-word and not be racist. I'm sorry! Isn't that kind of stupid? It's the about asinine-est thing I ever heard: "I use racial slurs, but I'm not racist, I just want to sound cool?" And that really bothers me, my feeling toward people that use racial slurs. I even have friends that I knew in high school that would draw swastikas on things just for fun.

The illogic of using racial slurs while claiming to not be racist made her gesture wildly; she could hardly remain seated in her chair in my office as she relayed such stories.

Madeline also couldn't bear to be mistaken for or silently associated with White racist people. With measured anger, she called out White people, including herself by saying "we," for their sense of entitlement to privilege:

> And then, it just makes me wonder more why White-supremacist groups really need to get together – I mean, what more do they want? We have the most dolls. We're pictured most in advertising. We have the most music. We have our own genres of music. Because, it's probably a pretty good generalization to say, there aren't that many Black country singers. We have our own everything. White people have all the jobs too. White people will generally have the best jobs. So I don't understand that. But I do understand why all the other people hate us. I'm really starting to understand that. And I feel bad too, because you go places, and then people don't like you because they generalize you into this group of terrible White people. And that's not very cool either.

Madeline simultaneously resisted and rejected privilege, taking responsibility for benefitting from it but also challenging it, trying to deflate the illusion of a historically established meritocracy, but also expressing her sense of betrayal by people who looked like her.

Yet she knew she was also culpable. Repeatedly she returned in the interview to her shock that she had never considered the depth of her privilege until reading Peggy McIntosh's famous list of white privileges:

> I never understood, other than for, like, status reasons–like White people get better jobs–why people of different ethnic backgrounds don't like us. Like, I never

> understood that until I read that list. I never understood that this world is being made for White people. It's the make-up, it's the clothes, it's the Barbie dolls. I'm sorry, but all the Black dolls that you will ever find are never made as good as Barbie. And I don't even think they have Mexican or Latino dolls anywhere. They don't even get dolls. Like, I never really noticed that before, but I think it helped everyone in the class because lots of people talked about that. It helped everyone in the class see why other groups resent White people.

Madeline painfully embodied this resentment but it would be oversimplification to describe her feelings as self-hate. It wasn't that she didn't want to be a White person; she loved her Irish side too. But while some of her classmates, like Roberta tried to become raceless when faced with culpability for White privilege, Madeline found intellectual and emotional spaces in the identity she was constructing for being and living as both-and.

Although diversity specialist Kerry Rockquemore and sociologist David Brunsma are writing about Black-White biracial people, their recall of Anzaldua's "border identity" seems to fit Madeline and her Middle Eastern ethnic identity. Defining a border identity as "one that lies between predefined social categories" (42), Roquemore and Brunsma explain that biracial people, and I'm arguing people who strongly experience their ethnic identity, seek recognition for a status that others find elusive and ephemeral:

> Meaning lies in their location of in-betweeness, and this unique status serves to ground their racial identity. Mixed-race people who understand being biracial as a border identity don't consider themselves to be either black or white but instead, incorporate both blackness and whiteness into a unique hybrid category of self-reference. One respondent explained that it was not only being on the border of socially defined categories but also experiencing the border status itself that brought with it an additional dimension. (Rockquemore and Brunsma 42)

Continuing to apply Roquemore and Brunsma's analysis, Madeline's border was between a "master status" (84) of White and a non-dominant identity, even derided, ethnic identity rather than a phenotype. Admittedly, this difference is complicated by the mitigating effects of her apparent Whiteness in at least two ways: (1) she identified more strongly with her Middle Eastern identity than her White identity, and (2) she often wanted to reject the White identity. When she sought validation from others for her chosen border identity, she often did not get it because they did not see or give importance to her ethnic identity, leaving her unvalidated except by her high school friend group. Thus she suffered what Roquemore and Brunsma term "an internalized social dislocation because of its continual oscillation between having its self-understanding validated by some and unvalidated by others" (45), leaving her "in a nebulous, marginal, and unresolved state with regard to [her] racial identity" (93). Again, though Rockquemore and Brunsma are speaking of skin color, their research on biracial border identity rings true for Madeline's efforts to be validated by others: "What does seem to influence their validation, not surprisingly, is how they perceive others' perception of their appearance (i.e. their socially mediated appearance)" (94). Thus for Madeline, clothing and her proclamation of her politics served as crucial public markers for an identity that is not as immediately obvious to others as a different skin color would be.

Ability to Name the Frame and Its Injury

With so little help from her peers, teachers, co-workers, and community, the class and her college experience had brought Madeline to another place where she encountered and began to name the features of what Feagin calls "the white racial frame," mentioned earlier. Madeline felt it her obligation to call out others on their lack of understanding of the chasm between the White world and those who lived lives in non-dominant identities. To her it was clear that we everyone lives in a land where White people are "willfully ignorant or very misinformed" (Feagin 3) about Madeline and other people of color. Madeline knew the data that evidences the White racial frame both empirically and experientially and often made it part of her arguments in class and in her essays. This White racial frame is the direct source of Madeline's frustration with her White classmates. As expressed in her interviews, she repeatedly struggled to fathom other students' lack of awareness of their own racial blindness, its logic and lack of empathy or understanding:

"It bothered me then, but it bothers me a lot more now – just that ignorance that I guess I understand now, of people, and how much they don't care, and they don't care to know that they're ignorant. They're ignorant and they don't care to be educated otherwise, and that really upsets me." To her, their ignorance felt deliberate and personal, which cut to the core of Madeline's hurt and alienation.

Madeline actually was not alone in that. Students of color often complain that their more privileged and often White classmates and teachers do not recognize the legitimacy of their feelings of subtle and blatant discrimination, alienation, and trauma from daily microaggressions. Sue and associates define "microaggression" as "brief, everyday exchanges that send denigrating messages to people of color because they belong to a racial minority group" (Sue et al. 273), Also sometimes called "microinequities," the "pattern of being overlooked, underrespected, and devalued because of one's race or gender" is "often unconsciously delivered in the form of subtle snubs or dismissive looks, gestures, and tones" (Sue et al., 273). In another article, Sue and Constantine describe the prevalence and impact of microagression, such as Madeline suffered:

> Microaggressive exchanges are so pervasive and automatic in daily conversations and interactions that they are often dismissed and glossed over as being innocent and innocuous. They are, nevertheless, extremely damaging to persons of color because microaggressions impair classroom performance and workplace productivity by creating emotional turmoil and depleting psychological resources. (137)

Subtle or overt, unintended or intentional, microaggressions cause many problems for students of color, including Madeline. I now believe her social and academic turmoil was directly due to the kind of microaggressions that Wing and his associates have studied.

Another race researcher team, sociologists Leslie Houts Picca and Joe Feagin, have documented the mechanism of microaggression is to operate in almost guerrilla fashion, covertly, often behind-the-scenes in "backstage" settings. Participants in the "backstage" think they are in a same-race but often are not actually, as Houts Picca and Feagin have shown. Hundreds of college student racial event diaries "reveal the networking character of the moments when many racist actions in the backstage are likely to be performed," providing "the critical communicative threads that bind all-white groups together" (113). As part of a multi-university study, students reported stories of racist jokes in apparently all-White settings, such as one participant's report of her White boyfriend's experience with his construction company co-workers:

> He told me about some of the jokes they like to tell, which insult women and black people. I asked him if he laughed and he said, "Of course I did, they were funny jokes." I thought this was bizarre because my boyfriend isn't racist in the least, although he is also of southern upbringing; yet he can laugh at jokes with racial or sexist content. When I asked him if he thought it was OK to make fun of black people or belittle women, he smartly answered no in fear of me ripping into him. What was most interesting to me is that I know he would never listen to or tell jokes like that unless he was in front of this particular group of friends. (113)

Not only do these backstage racist interactions set the norm, they sometimes directly victimize members of the crowd who, like Madeline or her classmate Annabelle's boyfriend, as mentioned in another chapter, appear White but also have non-White lineage. Thus, what may seem oversensitivity by people of color to language choices, particularly among friends in an apparently same-race setting is, in fact, a well-justified objection to the thoughtlessness, lack of critical consciousness, and pervasive everyday racism in the lives of those, like Madeline, who are more attuned. Such racist offenses are the adhesive, a kind of "social bond" among White people, a kind of White club against the Other, the outsider (Houts Picca and Feagin 112).

Further, psychologist Arthur Blume and his associates locate the impact of microaggression particularly at predominantly White universities, like Madeline's, with devastating effect:

> …[C]ollege students of color experience racial and ethnic microaggressions at significantly higher levels than European American students while being educated in historically White institutions. Furthermore, the study results suggest that college students of color who experience greater numbers of microaggressions may be at increased risks for higher anxiety and underage binge alcohol use as well as the aversive consequences of drinking alcohol. (49)

Such psychological and emotional damage has implications for students' ability to succeed in college and, ultimately, in life. Naming this injury "vicarious traumatization," psychologist Monica Williams explained to *New York Times* reporter Jenna Wortham that race-based trauma should be recognized in psychology's diagnostic manual (DSM) as "pathological, which means it is a disorder that we can assess and treat" (qtd. in Wortham). Both directly and indirectly, the message Madeline got from her classmates and even her teachers was that she was different, an outsider, from another world. They told her repeatedly that her looks and her ideas were not the norm, not once or twice but as the rule. I am not a therapist nor was I even Madeline's academic advisor, but she did relate to me repeated negative encounters with faculty and staff whom she felt did not listen to or respect her opinions and politics. At least partly as a result, Madeline took much longer than her peers to finish her degree, having stopped out at least once and spent much time resisting the guidance of her major advisor on her final thesis when she returned to school.

Thus, the hurt happens over and over. The injury of racism is repeated and reinforced by the actions of admittedly racist but also, most painfully, well-meaning people who believe themselves knowledgeable, fair and unbiased, including myself. People often do not "get" where Madeline or others like her are coming from or even recognize who they are, judging them by their appearance and the color of their politics, unwilling to credit their identity however it is constructed or the passions and voluble, challenging perspectives that emerge from and probably sustain them in their struggle. Teachers often don't give them time, space, or scaffolded learning experiences that support their development. Educators often don't challenge their White peers, White teachers, or institutional features that benefit Whiteness. I believe these failures are often because many teachers do not know another way but it's also because these issues are very close to home in ways they also have not found support to explore and understand.

The personal insight, that I too participated in misunderstanding Madeline, is a realization I only came to in writing this chapter. As the adage says, our students are truly are teachers! During the class and interviews, especially when her talk ran long with repeated protestations of her sympathy with people of color rather than Whites, I did not hear her racial identification. To me she was a young, overzealous White girl trying to make up for her sense of White guilt. It's apparent to me now that my own sense of guilt was distorting my vision.

I see now that rather than a defensive White girl who was trying to work out her liberal politics in discomfiting ways, she was actually trying to establish a new country, to bring us all to the land of "collective liberation" (Wise *Speaking* 357) where

> … however much we have caused damage, the fact that we can, if we choose, fight to undo the damage, to make amends, to repair a broken world, still matters. And if it is that—and *only that*—which separates us from the other creatures in this world, then who are we to fail in that solitary endeavor? How can we refuse to do the one thing that really makes us special and sets us apart? How can we walk the road of silence and collaboration and yet justify to ourselves the oxygen that, in so doing, we thieve from others who could put it to more productive use? (Wise *Speaking* 358)

This was what Madeline was trying to say. She suffered and often didn't succeed socially or academically. Her life felt messy, disorganized, unmoored at times. But she bravely persisted in her racial literacy project. She deeply felt and came to name herself as an anti-racist, an identity integral to her living her multiracial ethnic identity with integrity.

Students who are members of minority groups are struggling to find their way through education and life preparation just as any student does, but they are also fighting a lonely battle against the social and institutional tide, including their teachers' ability to hear and see them fully, understanding them and their needs without bias. While every student must ultimately do her own learning, the teacher's job is to provide help and support instead of a tidal wave of opposition and denial that grows out of their unwillingness to do their own homework. Teachers must catch up and do the work. Education needs to do better.

Madeline's story is about how for students whose racial identity is not clear to the observer, "difference" projects to others in many complex ways as resistant, obstructionist and perhaps temperamental or self-centered, even performative or guilty. But the observer can only see or hear what her own biases allow. The observer-teacher often cannot recognize or fully grasp the experience of isolation, disrespect and microaggression, resulting in profound student injury and the silencing of voices that clearly have more to say than the dominant norm can provide.

What I Wish I Had Said

The question, "Has anyone had a different experience?" is powerful because it directly draws students into a reckoning of their own experience and emotional attachments to their past understanding that they often find is incomplete. I like to use this question after the questions, "What is your story (behind that reaction or belief?) Where did it come from?" Those questions first allow students space to examine their own identity, its roots and emotional overlays. The question I associate with Madeline, "Has anyone had a different experience?" eases them into other people's narratives, helping students gravitate towards compassion and an understanding of The Other without feeling that they have lost their own identity. Having told their own story, they have room cognitively and emotionally for another's story. The skill to take another's perspective is part of "the developmental capacity of interdependence," a later stage of self-authorship in Baxter Magolda's student development model, discussed in Annabell's chapter.

Education professor Jane Bolgatz proposes raising slightly different questions that have the same effect of helping students to imagine the situation from a different perspective:

> Reactions to racial differences are tough to tackle, particularly when they are not articulated. Sometimes we can address them head-on. I can ask what difference it

> makes that my students are talking with a White teacher. Do they think we would talk differently if there were any Arab Americans, Whites, and so on in our class? (111)

Like Madeline's question, Bolgatz's queries introduce new information that engages students' personal experience or expertise but moves them a step beyond and outside it to discover new insights.

At the same time that the question "Has anyone had a different experience" awakens (White) students to other's lives, it provides a moment to recognize and legitimize the identity, perspective, and experience of people of color in the room, a countervailing note to the high number of microaggressions that they suffer from White students and faculty (Rivera et al.; Sue *Microaggressions in Everyday 137–159*; Watkins et al.). Students of color often bear the burden of microaggression in the classroom simply by witnessing the White students' stories, as Madeline's interviews illustrate. Centering their stories in classroom discussion could shift that harmful dynamic for them even as it educates the White students.

When Madeline was in my class, I did in fact repeatedly ask, "Has anyone had a different experience?" One of the struggles with that particular situation, though, was that she was one of only two people of color in the room, the other of whom was less willing to speak out. As I said, Madeline was a fighter emboldened by what she framed as the spiteful ignorance of others. At times it was hard to make room for anyone else in the discussion once she began. The trick in using this question is then to steer to follow-up questions that return the group's attention to the text and thus connect everyone's personal experiences and emotions on the floor to the contextual information provided by the reading, film or other text at hand.

The point of the question, "Has anyone had a different experience?" is to ensure that students consider the evidence and emotion outside of their own, particularly if they are White. With that question they (and teachers) gain an accessible, easy-to-remember tool for deconstructing race and racism in our society by simultaneously subjectively personalizing and objectively stepping outside of a potentially explosive racial encounter and move into real problem-solving.

Learning to recognize and understand differences among students (and being willing to take on the task) is a vital skill in effective pedagogy, particularly one that intends to enact greater social justice in the classroom and the world. This is a daunting project for even the most heroic of teachers, particularly when she senses a lack of support from her colleagues and/or her institution. In the next chapter, I look at some paths into that project that might make it a little more manageable by connecting teachers to the broader community of classroom social justice strategists and approaches.

Works Cited

Apfelbaum, Evan P. et al. "Seeing Race and Seeming Racist? Evaluating Strategic Colorblindness in Social Interaction." *Journal of Personality and Social Psychology*, vol. 95, no. 4, 2008, pp. 918–932.

Baxter Magolda, Marcia B. and Patricia M. King. *Learning Partnerships: Theory and Models of Practice to Educate for Self-Authorship*. Stylus, 2004.

Blume, Arthur W. et al. "The Relationship of Microaggressions with Alcohol Use: Anxiety among Ethnic Minority College Students in a Historically White Institution." *Cultural Diversity and Ethnic Minority Psychology*, vol. 18, no. 1, 2012, pp. 45–54, EBSCOhost.

Bolgatz, Jean. *Talking Race in the Classroom*. Teachers College Press, 2005.

Butler, Bethonie. "The Creators of Thug Kitchen Are White. Does It Matter?" *The Washington Post*, The Washington Post, 30 Sept. 2014, Arts and Entertainment.

Dawkins, Marcia Alesan. "Close to the Edge: The Representational Tactics of Eminem." *The Journal of Popular Culture*, vol. 43, no. 3, 2010, pp. 463–485, EBSCOhost.

Duncan, Patti. "Decentering Whiteness: Resisting Racism in the Women's Studies Classroom." *Race in the College Classroom: Pedagogy and Politics*, edited by Bonnie TuSmith and Maureen T. Reddy. Rutgers University Press, 2002, pp. 40–50.

Feagin, Joe R. *The White Racial Frame: Centuries of Racial Framing and Counter-Framing*. Routledge, 2010.

George, Mark Patrick. *Race Traitors, Exploring the Motivation and Action of White Antiracists*. Dissertation, University of New Mexico, 2004. Sociological Abstracts, CSA, Union Institute & University, doi:DA3129634 UMI, Ann Arbor, MI; 28 December 2005.

Harro, Bobbie. "The Cycle of Socialization." *Readings for Diversity and Social Justice*, edited by Maurianne Adams et al. Routledge, 2000, pp. 15–21.

Houts Picca, Leslie and Joe R. Feagin. *Two-Faced Racism: Whites in the Backstage and the Frontstage*. Routledge, 2007.

Huot, Brian. *(Re)Articulating Assessment: Writing Assessment for Teaching and Learning*. Utha State University Press, 2002. eBook, 1 June 2007.

Johnson, Kirk et al. "Rachel Dolezal, in Center of Storm, Is Defiant: 'I Identify as Black'." *The New York Times*, The New York Times, 16 June 2015. http://www.nytimes.com, 29 June 2015.

McIntosh, Peggy. "White Privilege and Male Privilege: A Personal Account of Coming to See Correspondences through Work in Women's Studies" *Working Paper*, Center for Research on Women, Wellesley College, 1988.

Rivera, David P. et al. "Microaggressions and the Life Experience of Latina/O Americans." *Microaggressions and Marginality: Manifestation, Dynamics, and Impact*, edited by Derald Wing Sue. John Wiley & Sons, Inc., 2010, pp. 59–83.

Rockquemore, Kerry Ann and David L. Brunsma. *Beyond Black: Biracial Identity in America*. Sage Publications, 2002.

Sue, Derald Wing. *Microaggressions in Everyday Life: Race, Gender, and Sexual Orientation*. John Wiley & Sons, Inc., 2010.

—. *Race Talk and the Conspiracy of Silence*. John Wiley & Sons, Inc., 2015.

Sue, Derald Wing et al. "Racial Microaggressions in Everyday Life: Implications for Clinical Practice." *American Psychologist*, vol. 62, no. 4, 2007, pp. 271–286, EBSCOhost Integrated Search.

Sue, Derald Wing and Madonna G. Constantine. "Racial Microaggressions as Instigators of Difficult Dialogues on Race: Implications for Student Affairs Educators and Students." *The College Student Affairs Journal*, vol. 26, no. 2, 2007, pp. 136–143, EBSCOhost Integrated Search.

Tatum, Beverly Daniel. *"Why Are All the Black Kids Sitting Together in the Cafeteria?" And Other Conversations About Race*. Basic Books, 2003.

The CERCL Writing Collective. *Breaking Bread, Breaking Beats*. Fortress Press, 2014.

Thompson, Craig J. and Diana L. Haytko. "Speaking of Fashion: Consumers' Uses of Fashion Discourses and the Appropriation of Countervailing Cultural Meanings." *Journal of Consumer Research*, vol. 24, 1997, pp. 15–42, EBSCOhost.

Twine, France Winddance. "White Antiracism in Multiracial Families." *Off-White: Readings on Power, Privilege, and Resistance*, edited by Michelle Fine et al., 2nd edition. Routledge, 2004, pp. 395–410.

Watkins, Nicole L. et al. "Black Undergraduates' Experiences with Perceived Racial Microaggressions in Predominately White Colleges and Universities." *Microaggressions and Marginality: Manifestations, Dynamics, and Impact*, edited by Derald Wing Sue. John Wiley & Sons, Inc., 2010, pp. 25–57.

Wise, Tim. "Mimicry Is Not Solidarity: Of Allies, Rachel Dolezal and the Creation of Antiracist White Identity." Tim Wise: Antiracist Essayist, Author and Educator. N.p. 14 June 2015. Web.

—. *Speaking Treason Fluently: Anti-racist Reflections from an Angry White Male*. Soft Skull, 2008.

Wortham, Jenna. "Racism's Psychological Toll." *The New York Times Magazine*, online edition, The New York Times Company, 24 June 2015.

· 7 ·

NEXT STEPS

We do very little as a profession to help each other sustain our moments of realization and honesty. While writing the previous chapter and trying to face the truth of my complicity in silencing Madeline, I, a White liberal, came across this cogent, very personal indictment of White liberals in an article entitled "Racial Microaggressions in Everyday Life" by a team of pscyhologists headed by Derald Wing Sue, whom I greatly respect. I awkwardly include all of their citations so that readers may experience the quote firsthand:

> It appears that modern and symbolic racism are most closely associated with political conservatives, who disclaim personal bigotry by strong and rigid adherence to traditional American values (individualism, self-reliance, hard work, etc.), whereas aversive racism is more characteristic of White liberals (Dovidio & Gaertner, 1996, 2000). Aversive racists, according to these researchers, are strongly motivated by egalitarian values *as well as antiminority feelings*. Their egalitarian values operate on a conscious level while *their antiminority feelings are less conscious and generally covert*" (Devos & Banaji 2005). (272 emphasis added).

Just days earlier I had explained to my mother that my motivation for doing this work comes from my realization that I have been afraid of Black people on some deep level even though she and my dad had worked hard to teach me otherwise. I hadn't named this aversive racism, but it is.

The fact is, the damage of my kind of racism is more subtle but perhaps even more devastating than overt acts of racism, as Sue et al., go on to argue:

> Ironically, it has been proposed that the daily common experiences of racial aggression that characterize aversive racism may have significantly more influence on racial anger, frustration, and self-esteem than traditional overt forms of racism (Solorzano, ceja, & Yosso, 2000). Furthermore, the invisible nature of acts of aversive racism prevents perpetrators from realizing and confronting (a) their own complicity in creating psychological dilemmas for minorities and (b) their role in creating disparities in employment, health care, and education. (Sue et al. 272)

The awful truth is that we White people are all racist, whether we want to be or not. We breathe the smog of racism, as Beverly Daniel Tatum names it (6). We battle our private aversions, thinking we are progressive as we try to do better things in our classrooms. But we all participate in the system, excuse our shortfalls and oversights, and try to reconcile our theory with our praxis. After all, we are only human. But the result is the silencing, and worse, of students like Madeline.

As shamed as I felt in writing her chapter, I was fortunate to have had Madeline as a voluble, highly engaged student. She helped me see that we—teachers, institutions—need to do more to unlearn racism and avoid the kind of misjudgment and identity damage I have described here. Writing this chapter and revisiting Madeline's interviews have helped me reform my understanding and appreciation for Madeline's form of resistance to the pedagogy. I am only now understanding that her forms of resistance—rejection of her peers, avoidance of in-depth research on her topic, procrastination on her projects, endless talking and story-telling—were all in some ways a justified effort at survival in a system that was only going to paint her as less than, regardless of her outcomes.

We need to do more for students like Madeline. Not everyone will have a Madeline to help out as she helped me, and I only wish someone had helped me before I met her so that I could have heard her voice more clearly and understood more fully the part the university and I played in reifying racist attitudes and structures. We must stop learning these lessons individually over and over again and build supports for ourselves and our students to do this hard work. We must dream bigger than we have up to now and face the work ahead better equipped to help ourselves and each other.

So how do we do this? While the "What I Wish I Had Said" sections of this book provide some ideas of strategies tried and others that seem good in retrospect, the following discussion provides some additional thoughts and resources.

Overcoming the White Racial Frame and Our White Fragility

Previously I referred to the concept of the White racial frame that Feagin has used as an analytical and activist research tool to call out White supremacy in our history and culture, including among our students . Education researchers Coburn, Toure and Yamashita have pointed to the usefulness of the White racial frame in identifying leadership shortfalls among school administrators (Coburn et al.). An awareness of the frame could be useful to individual instructors in critiquing their own classroom dynamics, curricular design, assessment and grading policies.

Notably, though, faculty could achieve a much greater impact by using the White racial frame on a departmental, college, or university level to expose and remedy the presence of White supremacy in all its hiding places: admissions, hiring, promotion, institutional organization and governance, professional development, budget and fundraising, student affairs, and all other institutional components. There are organizations and consultants who will assist that undertaking, which could conceivably be supported by federal Title III funds as an institutional improvement project that ultimately increases faculty, staff, and student diversity and the sustainability of the university. For a DIY approach, see "Hale's Inventory for Assessing an Institution's Commitment to Multicultural Programming;" consult the local YWCA (formerly the Young Women's Christian Association) which often provides institutional racism assessments; or learn more about the W.K. Kellogg Foundation, which also promotes racial equity and institutional change in many projects it supports. This is not as exhaustive a list as a Google search will show. It's also informative to ask colleagues in the field and sister institutions for referrals. Obviously this is an ambitious project but one that could be proposed and advocated for by a "woke" department or college, beginning with a faculty member like yourself.

But how do faculty get past their White fragility, mentioned earlier, to arrive at "woke?" Di Angelo's work in White fragility hits home for many because it calls out, names, and challenges White people to do better than holding to their fear of being found out as racist. The last chapter of her *White*

Fragility: Why It's So Hard For White People to Talk About Racism narrates a recent story of her own misstep in dismissing some professional work done by an African American colleague and how she sought to repair that relationship: She apologized, acknowledged her fault, did not ask for comfort as a normally good White person or make excuses for herself, and asked for public feedback the next time she (inevitably) makes a mistake like that. Such mistakes, she says, are part of the risk of being genuinely engaged with people whose lived experiences are different from their own very White lives, steeped in supremacy. The alternative to making mistakes is to be silent and segregated, which are no longer acceptable paths. DiAngelo suggests some "transformed" responses when someone calls out a person's unintentional offense:

- I appreciate this feedback.
- This is very helpful.
- It's my responsibility to resist defensiveness and complacency.
- This is hard, but also stimulating and important.
- Oops!
- It is inevitable that I have this pattern. I want to change it.
- It's personal, but not strictly personal.
- I will focus on the message and not the messenger.
- I need to build my capacity to endure discomfort and bear witness to the pain of racism.
- I have some work to do. (142)

DiAngelo says such responses are operating out of a "transformed" paradigm, as opposed to the dominant supremacist one usually used by White people, aka Feagin's White racial frame. She also provides a rich list of assumptions that would mark a transformed environment, including, "Giving us white people feedback on our racism is risky for people of color, so we can consider the feedback a sign of trust," and "Racism hurts (even kills) people of color 24–7. Interrupting it is more important than my feelings, ego, or self-image" (142–43).

When people ask Di Angelo what to do about racism and their White fragility, she writes, "[T]he first thing I ask is, 'What has enabled you to be a full, educated, professional adult and not know what to do about racism?' It is a sincere question. How have we managed not to know, when the information is all around us? When people of color have been telling us for years?" (144). Here is a summary of her customizable path:

1. Do whatever kept you from knowing—get educated, get to know people of color, get out of your bubble, etc.—whatever has caused you not to know what to do about your fragility.
2. Adopt the transformed paradigm assumptions that she details.
3. Seek out information outside of White circles, "break with apathy," care enough to go after whatever will help you change.
4. Talk to other White people about race and racism, "break the silence."
5. Act out of integrity, not inappropriate guilt, desire for comfort or reassurance. (142–52).

Di Angelo closes with this striking admonition: "To continue reproducing racial inequality, the system only needs white people to be really nice and carry on, smile at people of color, be friendly across race, and go to lunch together on occasion" (153). She is saying what White people already know in their hearts: they must do more.

Learning from and with Inoue

Asao Inoue smiled as he fired the first shots in a microrevolution at the 2019 Conference on College Composition and Communication (4Cs) in Pittsburgh, PA. But even those who were not there, including myself, heard his volley. His keynote address as convention chair, "How Do We Language So People Stop Killing Each Other, Or What Do we Do About White Language Supremacy?" opened, no pun intended, with a trigger warning that he planned to be honest with us out of love for us good people, but "it may hurt" and that he needed us to be patient with him (Inoue 2). Why? Another smile. Because, basically, as he went on to argue over the next several minutes, we English writing teachers, whether we are White or people of color, insist on the continued dominance of Standard Edited American English (SEAE), which ultimately enables White supremacy.

I don't know if people in the room stopped breathing when they grasped his message within the first minutes of his speech. In the videotape, I didn't hear any audible gasps or outcry at that point. But as I read the text, I felt punched in the stomach. And as I revisited that moment on video, I felt particular pain at his smile as he said, "I also ask many of you to be patient as I first address my colleagues of color, but the fact that I must ask for your patience to do this is evidence of the White supremacy that even we, conscientious teachers of writing, are saturated in" (Inoue 2). Having laid bare all our fragile

White souls and implicated the people of color too, he then proceeded to depict the metaphorical "steel cage of White supremacy" that confines and ultimately kills non-White people. In the next breath he implicated his own colleagues of color (as well as himself) for having participated in the system and benefitted from such capitulation. Within minutes of his start, Inoue had charged us all with high crimes, and I suspect we were all feeling the shame of the accusation, especially as it confirmed the suspicions about our practices that we thought we had sufficiently hid from the world under the guise of professionalism.

If you don't have this feeling, I challenge you to read his words and feel differently.

Actually, don't.

I'd also like to ask your patience to hear him out without defensiveness. I cannot tell if the power of his language is inherent to his ideas or if they just happened to play on my White guilt and secret fear of incompetence. Judging from the outcry and eventual implosion of the very widely subscribed Writing Program Administrator's List-serve, which you also may have witnessed shortly after the March 2019 conference, I suspect many other writing teachers were feeling as targeted as I did (and still do), whether they were White or people of color. We all teach the dominant discourse in Standard Edited American English (SEAE), which from Inoue's perspective, is our pride and shame. As his title says, it is the language responsible for our killing each other.

In terms of next steps in our response to the racism we allow and that which, Inoue charges, we create and sustain, my suggestion here is that we (1) take in his important, damning argument and (2) find a way to respond meaningfully. First, his argument.

Referring to a figurative steel cage of White Supremacy that has resulted in actual prison bars incarcerating Black men "at five times that of their White peers, and Latinos at twice the rate of Whites" (Inoue 2), Inoue first addresses his colleagues of color in the audience, saying "the ways we judge language form some of the steel bars around our students and ourselves—we too maintain White supremacy, even as we fight against it in other ways" (Inoue 3). He contends that there is a "market of White language preferences in schools" (Inoue 4) that marks, controls, and limits the way we name and create our realities: "Who has been allowed to name people, places, things, the processes of writing and revision, theories of rhetoric? Who has named your sky? Who has named your writing, my friends? Who has named your pedagogies? Who has named your ways of judging language, my colleagues of color?" (Inoue 5)

He is talking about me. I am the one in my classroom that teaches the standard and holds students to it. And it is clearly a White standard. Probably like many teachers, I have known and felt uncomfortable at times about this for a long time. As doctrinaire as I had been taught to be, as picky about grammar, style, organization, logic, rhetorical strategy, tone, usage, word choice that defined my role as arbiter of the language of the realm, I have always been a little queasy about the sometimes devastating effect of my judgment of others' writing. It sometimes felt arbitrary, especially when a colleague could justify an entirely opposite evaluation.

And then, I note the undeniable racial breakdown of those that benefited from my assessment and those that were penalized harshly with, no exaggeration, life-changing impact, such as students who failed the placement writing sample and were put in a developmental class with grammar tutoring that met no requirements and added to their loan burden; who failed the developmental writing course (again) that cost hefty tuition dollars but awarded no college credit, even when passed; who scraped by with a "mercy" grade just before graduating in a major they didn't ask for but that permitted their resultant low GPA and damaged self-concept, and who knows what consequences beyond. That's why Inoue's words have such sting when he says of my Whiteness and attachment to SEAE: "You can be a problem even when you try not to be. Sit and lament in your discomfort and its sources. Search. If our goal is a more socially just world, we don't need more good people. We need good changes, good structures, good work that makes good changes, structures, and people" (7).

Inoue's words set the stage for one of my recent adult students, an African American man I'll call James, who is probably in his fifties. James had endured much in his life in Detroit as an autoworker, handyman, caregiver for an elderly aunt, advisor (and loan officer) to numerous nieces and nephews, anchor and role model to an extended family struggling to build good lives in sometimes tenuous neighborhoods. James chose to be in my grant writing class in his last semester before he finally earned his B.A. in religious studies. In my class he endured a student work group of four very young undergrad women, three of them White, one Black. None of these young women understood his experience or its value. They did not recognize his authority or approve of his grammar. They decided they would be good, cooperative students and just work around him. They failed to include him in their planning for a group project, ignored his editing suggestions, rewrote his sections without permission or consultation, and insisted on communicating by text, even after he told them that he doesn't text.

He complained to me. I sent him back to the group to work it out. Separately I spoke to the ostensible leader and told her she needed to try harder to include him and to hear what he had to offer. When the first of two group writing projects still did not turn out well and was graded as such, they all came to me in distress. I ultimately agreed to a rewrite so they could change their dynamic a little. In the second group writing project, after some loud compliments from me about the high quality of James's work on the budget section of the grant and another shout-out I made to him as we problem-solved other students' difficulties with that writing, the rest of the class, including his group, started to turn to him for advice on that and other sections. Ultimately, James and his group earned their A. It seemed a small miracle. I was fairly sure he and I had done well together, overcome some hurdles, but part of me still kept composing justification for the high number of A's in that class generally. I kept expecting to be challenged by the program director or department chair; I wasn't entirely confident in my handling of the situation.

There was another layer of interaction with James that I also want to consider in the light of Inoue's speech. James was not a polished or highly experienced writer. His grammar included many errors when evaluated as SEAE, and while I do not weight grammar heavily, my practice has been to name the kinds of errors and refer students to the writing center tutors for some remediation. At times I have awarded extra credit for those visits in the hope that students will be motivated to learn how to fix their mistakes independently. I didn't offer extra credit this semester but I referred him to the tutors repeatedly. He expressed frustration at the number of times I did that, saying he had fixed the mistakes and that we had a simple difference of opinion. He'd come to me privately and questioned me on sections where I said his word usage was incorrect; he insisted his word choice meant the same thing as the alternative I offered. I eventually learned that he was not consulting the tutors but relying on Microsoft Word's grammar checker, which could not identify or offer remedies for the words or phrases I had marked for attention. At times he would use words that were sophisticated beyond everyday usage but were not quite the right technical meaning, such as "information" for "evaluation." (Examples are similar, not actual.) At other times, the words just did not work well together to convey meaning, such as "Effectiveness and efficiency to training this project will bring faith in returns." He would make changes but under protest that he was already saying what needed to be said.

Eventually, he won me over and I think we met somewhere in the middle. I don't know if that was right or racist but I contend it was an ethical judgment. My standard moved from technically correct SEAE to assessment of whether or not his argument and case for support would be taken seriously by the readers who determined the grant awards. As a long-time grant writer who has been in the position of serving as such a reader, I felt they *would* take him seriously, despite the occasional misused word or the SEAE grammar error. James did communicate the overall meaning with a clear passion for the cause and presented authentic evidence to support it.

Assessing James's work differently was my fledgling effort to evaluate his work for its own value, not in relation to the work of others in the class. Although I had not heard Inoue's words at the time, I know I was responding to my perception of the need he foregrounded in his speech:

> Again, let me compassionately urge you to sit in discomfort: If you use a single standard to grade your students' languaging, you engage in racism. You actively promote White language supremacy, which is the handmaiden to White bias in the world, the kind that kills Black men on the streets by the hands of the police through profiling and good ol' fashion prejudice. (11)

If the point is communication, hadn't James communicated? Though I am admittedly not comfortable in my answer yet, I must honestly say, "Yes!" His successful communication is the point, not my discomfort.

In making this case, Inoue, like DiAngelo, reaches back to Pierre Bourdieu's concept of "habitus" to justify this kind of assessment. He contends that "grading locally diverse students" must recognize and account for White social bias as part of the teacher's privilege,

> … likely part of the reason you are in front of the class in the first place. If we can confront such paradoxes in our judgements of language, in our *habitus*, then maybe some of the killing may stop. But first, we have to painfully reconcile our habits of judgement, and that means painfully reconciling the paradox between ourselves and our actions. As Bourdieu's term, *habitus*, makes clear, one's judgement is not simply one's own individual judgement of something. It is never simply an individual practice. It is consubstantial, interconnected, to the social world we live in. (Inoue 12)

White people's *habitus* unconsciously maintains White privilege, and, as DiAngelo explains, "We don't respond consciously to disequilibrium in the habitus; we respond unconsciously" (103). Faced with racial disequilibrium, White people will act to restore the social balance to their own favor. But

DiAngelo and Inoue are arguing that this social moment is when White people need to consciously intervene or interrupt the *habitus*.

In my classroom, I worked to model resistance to the unconscious responses and make them consciously anti-racist. My students who appeared in this book noticed their *habitus*, although that is not a term they would use to describe their unearned advantages. They realized that they were more comfortable talking in a predominantly White environment to a White teacher. They noticed just how White our class was and who was *not* there. They were aware of how disorienting and sometimes scary it was for them to consider the effects of policy like capital punishment that fell disproportionately on Black men, policy they had hitherto considered objectively designed and structured. They also felt how hard it was to feel silenced by teachers and classmates who had no idea of others' experience of discrimination and isolation.

I used to think of my classrooms as inclusive because I worked hard to make everyone feel welcome, comfortable and worthy. But I taught writing as having "correct" and "incorrect" grammar or attention to audience or organization or argument development across the board because those were the standards. I did not recognize the intolerance, lack of openness, and the White biases that are built into those standards. Even when I saw value in approaches outside of those White conventions, as in James's case, I still insisted that he needed to learn how to recognize his writing deficits, to find a buddy or a tutor who could earmark his errors to be sure that the (White) world would accept and understand him.

Inoue says, "We must stop justifying White standards of writing as a necessary evil. Evil in any form is never necessary. We must stop saying that we have to teach this dominant English because it's what students need to succeed tomorrow. They only need it because we keep teaching it!" (19). As James said to me near the end of the class when I emphasized yet again that he needed an editor-friend, he smiled and said that another teacher once told him, "You need to learn to write White." Still smiling, he said to me "I get it." And then I got it.

I am at the "Damned if you do, damned if you don't" stage, as Inoue described it. Apparently it's where my students of color have been all along. I don't know what to do at this point except to begin as I have with the compassionate listening and the questions I described in the rest of this book. Inoue himself identifies similar approaches:

- Employ "Deep listening" (Inoue 16) to be able to problematize the assumptions and the habitus of teaching and assessment.
- Listen, not to control and remake the students, but to affirm their existence as they are, not as "the Whitely Rex Harrison languaging Audrey Hepburn into existence when we know, ain't nothin' wrong with Audrey but Rex's judgements" (Inoue 17) referring to the musical version of George Bernard Shaw's *Pygmalion*, *My Fair Lady*.
- Use "Deep and mindful attending" to the "suchness of that person," as identified by the Buddhist monk Thich Nat Hanh, in order, Inoue says "to understand others without trying to control or change them" (Inoue 17).
- Apply all this to grading so that "Assessment might be a problem-posing process that continually attends to questions like: 'Do I understand you enough? Am I making you suffer? Please help me to read your languaging properly'" (Inoue 18).
- Make structural changes in our practice that enable/expect more listening and thinking time: "Part of my answer is that some must be silent, leave enough space between utterances, so that problematizing can happen … cutting the steel bars, altering the ecology, in which your biases function in your classrooms and communities" (Inoue 19).

As I experienced with my student James, I realize I am the one who must be silent more. And I am responsible for structuring the spaces in our class work and in the writing process that allow for students to say and for me to hear that an argument, a source, a way of framing or phrasing can communicate the point as well as or better than the SEAE or White convention.

As Inoue forecast, I'm not certain I'm ready for all of this. Apparently, there were others feeling the same or worse after his keynote in Pittsburgh. You may have witnessed the disastrous deterioration of civility and professionalism that occurred in the days after the conference on the Writing Program Administrators List-Serve. That list-serve is the premier virtual forum for composition instructors at all levels.

After several days, a brave group of list-serve members, the Writing Program Adminstrators' List-serve (WPA-L) Reimagining Working Group, volunteered to use collaborative documents to think through and flesh out possible participation guidelines, the idea of a moderation board, and some options for a name change. The intent is to encourage more diversity of voices that can enjoy more respectful, productive interchange among list-serve members. A subsequent vote on the drafts by 213 of the 4,344 subscribed members indicated the majority were in favor of adopting the new participation guidelines, operating with the support of a volunteer board with rotating membership, and retaining the current list-serve name, WPA-L (WPA-L Reimagining Working Group). It remains to be seen if the members can use this new format to accomplish the intended goals.

Similarly, I don't exactly know how to do the kinds of student-centered assessment that teaches the features and processes of written communication without belittling or silencing the historically minimized voices among us. I confess I don't know what this kind of teaching or assessment looks like, even though I own both of Inoue's books on the topic. (See Inoue, Asao & Mya Poe, Eds. *Race and Writing Assessment*, 2012; and Inoue, Asao, *Antiracist Writing Ecologies*, 2015.) Why have I only sampled them? Why am I hanging back? If I am to have any integrity in this work, it's time for me step it up because "What a sense of blind privilege it is to tell a starving person at your doorstep, in your house of plenty, in a land of abundance, that you just don't yet feel comfortable enough to share your food" (Inoue 20). Our (White) time is up. I think we all agree—our comfort is not the point.

Teaching Racial Literacy

Mara Grayson does have a way out of this dilemma. She is a member of the WPA-L Reimagining Group, Chair of the National Council of Teachers of English (NCTE) Jewish Caucus, and one of the founders of a new 4Cs special interest group on intersectionality. Her book *Teaching Racial Literacy: Reflective Practices for Critical Writing* is the book that I wish I had written or at least seen much earlier in my career. She validates many of the points that my book *Teaching and Race* makes because there is a considerable overlap between my approach of compassionate listening followed by critical challenge with her racial literacy framework, which she defines by building on Twine and Guinier.

Twine's case study of White mothers of biracial children identified the importance to Black children of "the provision of conceptual and discursive practices with which to understand the function(s) of race; access to Black social networks; and exposure to Black-produced media and significant symbols of Black struggles" (Grayson 5). Guinier broadened the concept of racial literacy to include other people of color as well, widening to include "'psychological, interpersonal, and structural dimensions' of race; and 'constantly interrogates the dynamic relationship among race, class, geography, gender, and other explanatory variables'" (qtd. in Grayson 5). In a racial literacy curriculum then, according to Grayson, "students read racially charged texts, engage in problem-solving group discussions, and use reflective writing to identify and respond to racial inequity" (6); this actually describes the curriculum I created in which racially themed readings, films, discussion, and writing engaged my students.

Grayson's text works well as follow-up to the case studies in *Teaching and Race* because she delineates the specific steps to structure the classroom communication dynamic, the curricular design, navigation of institutional politics, and personal racial identity study and self-care that teachers need to consider when they decide to build an anti-racist activist classroom experience. For example, she gives a quick-reference list of the desired communication activities (Share, Inquire, Listen actively, Acknowledge what others have said, Respond) in an easy-read box early in the book (Grayson 9) which might be useful to help instructors ease into a racial literacy curriculum.

When teachers are ready for a more in-depth consideration of how to teach racial literacy, they can consider her table of "Discursive Practices of Racial Literacy" that names and applies some relevant rhetorical concepts (positionality, authorial choice, critical thinking, textual representation, audience, voice, tone) that would help the instructor appropriately integrate racial literacy into the typical composition course and advocate for it to the department or dean (Grayson 10–11).

Subsequent chapters add pragmatic how-tos and justification for using the racial literacy curriculum to guide and respond to students much like the ones in this book. They could be used either piecemeal, again to ease into the racial literacy approach, or to flesh out a full curriculum. For example, part of the planning advice she gives in her second chapter includes another box on "Developing a Racial Literacy Practice to Become a Racial Literacy Educator" that could build instructor skill sets and confidence to engage students in classroom race talk. Grayson talks the instructor through considerations of how to manage local school culture and politics (19–22); how to avoid some of the pitfalls, such as the "black-white binary" (27); how to honestly and productively handle emotions that surface (her fifth chapter) including legitimizing and encouraging "minoritized" voices using "counterstorytelling" (65), and much more. In other words, Grayson's text is a layered primer in how to get started and then what to do next, making this entire project a very doable if still challenging approach to teaching as an anti-racist social justice activist.

Find a Buddy

Teaching can be lonely work, despite the fact that we practice it in a room full of students amidst numerous colleagues. It is especially lonely for those of us who work practically without institutional support or recognition of the chosen harder path of anti-racist teaching. The daily difficulty of not only teaching writing but paddling upstream against cultural and institutional resistance can be exhausting, discouraging, confusing, even heart-breaking. Being in the classroom regularly induces self-doubt and moral quandary.

That's why almost above all else, if teachers want to be sustainable, responsible, well-balanced educators in this very challenging approach, they must find a buddy and/or a community to support them. They need someone to help them problem-solve, question their assumptions, call out their biases (they will still be there!), and remind them of why they do this work. It felt like it took a long time for my department to understand and, I think, trust me. I joined a faculty writers group with much trepidation, feeling very out of step and behind as a late-in-life academic. But scholarship was a language my faculty colleagues understood. In the best tradition of writing to learn, I wrote to them about my anti-racist teaching struggles, feeling very vulnerable and exposed. Like the generous teacher-scholars they are, they helped me become a better advocate, scholar, and researcher and they came to understand what I was about. I feel very fortunate since this gift is not afforded everyone at the home institution.

But there is a whole community of us out there who will do the same for you, if you ask. Despite its recent difficulties, the Writing Program Administrators List-serve is a valuable meeting space and hopefully will become a useful, more equitable discussion forum in the coming years.

Conferences, particularly the Conference on College Composition and Communication will yield like-minded souls. Find the track that fits your interests. Find the teacher-scholars mentioned in this book, go to their sessions, become one of their groupies! Others there will very likely respond to your overtures for collegiality because they are all searching for the same. Anti-racist activist teaching has to grow out of community to be honest to its intentions or it risks repeating the same destructive patterns that have been the White-dominated tradition in the field of composition.

Closing Thoughts

When I began this book project several years ago, I was somewhat depressed about the potential of digging my way (our way) out of racism in the classroom. It's only one semester. We get so little support from our institutions and so much resistance from the students themselves, as well as our colleagues and communities at times. What difference can one teacher accomplish in the space of 48 hours in a 3-credit one-semester class? How can we undo centuries of tribalism, fear, greed, and hate? It is especially discouraging in our current political maelstrom which offers little vision of hope or integrity in this fight. How can we presume to have answers?

But at this end of the project, my hope has been restored. The students interviewed in this book gave me reason to keep looking for those answers. They led me to understand the power of compassionate listening and the importance of the critical challenge questions they embody. But overcoming our biases and learning to use our teaching as an anti-racist project is a tall order. The urgency of the need for this project must outweigh our privileged sense of a job-too-big-to-handle. What I have offered you in this chapter is a framework for personal development in DiAngelo's *White Fragility*; a lofty challenge to end institutionalized racism in our field in Inoue's speech; and a graduated curriculum redesign that embodies greater respect for each other in our teaching of language in Grayson's *Teaching Racial Literacy*.

What I have offered you in this book are four case studies of sincere and hard working students with various challenges and resistances that have handicapped them all. Their difficulties in race talk reflect typical shock, fear, denial, cognitive dissonance and disequilibrium, resistance and *habitus*, as well as their varying capacities to integrate a coherent positive racial identity in spite of the racist smog they breathe. They mark the terrible inequity, pain, and destruction inherent in all interactions and institutions in a racialized racist society. They also exemplify some of the challenges that fill the stress dreams of the teachers of such students. Often these teachers feel they cannot afford the time, energy, or personal risk it takes to confront classroom racism or to help students unlearn it.

In today's news was another overwhelming story of a tweet by our current president that taunted four new U.S. congresswomen, all women of color, to "Go back" to the countries they came from, even though three of the four are U.S.-born citizens (Sullivan). Such thinly coated racism is pervasive and, though condemned in some corners, often institutionally protected and lauded as patriotic, common-sense free speech. Teachers need the skills and support to address this kind of failure in human interaction if our society is to have any hope of honesty, integrity, clear thought, equity, justice and compassion in generations to come.

I hope the ideas, information and tools in this book can give you a starting point to make the kinds of changes you, your students, our field and our world want and need.

Best wishes.

Works Cited

Coburn, Cynthia E. et al. "Evidence, Interpretation, and Persuasion: Instructional Decision Making at the District Central Office." *Teacher's College Record*, vol. 111, no. 4, 2009, pp. 1115–1161.

DiAngelo, Robin. *White Fragility*. Beacon Press, 2018.

Feagin, Joe R. *The White Racial Frame: Centuries of Racial Framing and Counter-Framing*. Routledge, 2010.

Grayson, Mara Lee. *Teaching Racial Literacy: Reflective Practices for Critical Writing*. Rowman & Littlefield, 2018.

Hale, Frank W. "Hale's Inventory for Assessing an Institution's Commitment to Multicultural Programming." *What Makes Racial Diversity Work in Higher Education*, edited by Frank W. Hale, 1st edition. Stylus Publishing, 2004, pp. 307–317.

Inoue, Asao B. "How Do We Language So People Stop Killing Each Other, or What Do We Do About White Language Supremacy?." *Conference on College Composition and Communication*, Keynote address, 14 March 2019.

Sue, Derald Wing et al. "Racial Microaggressions in Everyday Life: Implications for Clinical Practice." *American Psychologist*, vol. 62, no. 4, 2007, pp. 271–286, EBSCOhost Integrated Search.

Sullivan, Eileen. "Trump's Tweet Was Condemned as Racist. His Response: No, They're Racists." *The New York Times*, The New York Times, 15 July 2019.

Tatum, Beverly Daniel. *"Why Are All the Black Kids Sitting Together in the Cafeteria?" And Other Conversations About Race*. Basic Books, 2003.

WPA-L Reimagining Working Group. "Outcome of Voting on Future of Wpa-L." edited by WPA-L Members, email, 12 July 2019.

INDEX OF AUTHORS

INDEX OF WORDS AND PHRASES

Studies in Composition and Rhetoric

Edited by Alice S. Horning

This series welcomes both individually-authored and collaboratively-authored books and monographs as well as edited collections of essays. We are especially interested in books that might be used in either advanced undergraduate or graduate courses in one or more of the following subjects: cultural or multicultural studies and the teaching of writing; feminist perspectives on composition and rhetoric; postmodernism and the theory and practice of composition; "post-process" pedagogies; values, ethics, and ideologies in the teaching of writing; information technology and composition pedagogy; the assessment of writing; authorship and intellectual property issues; and studies of oppositional discourse in the academy, particularly challenges to exclusionary or hegemonic conventions. We also seek proposals in the following areas: the role of autobiography and of identity issues in both writing and writing pedagogy; the influence of social context on composing; the relationship of composition and rhetoric to various disciplines and schools of thought; collaborative learning and peer tutoring; facilitating and responding to student writing; approaches to empowering marginalized learners; the role or status of composition studies within English studies and the academy at large; and the role or status of student writers within the fields of composition and English studies.

For additional information about this series or for the submission of manuscripts, please contact:

Peter Lang Publishing, Inc.
Acquisitions Department
29 Broadway
New York, NY 10006

To order other books in this series, please contact our Customer Service Department at:

peterlang@presswarehouse.com (within the U.S.)
order@peterlang.com (outside the U.S.)

or browse online by series at:

WWW.PETERLANG.COM